Praise for *Inside the Minds*

"Need-to-read inside information and analysis that will improve your bottom line - the best source in the business." – Daniel J. Moore, Member, Harris Beach LLP

"The Inside the Minds series is a valuable probe into the thought, perspectives, and techniques of accomplished professionals…" – Chuck Birenbaum, Partner, Thelen Reid & Priest

"Aspatore has tapped into a gold mine of knowledge and expertise ignored by other publishing houses." – Jack Barsky, Managing Director, Information Technology & Chief Information Officer, ConEdison *Solutions*

"Unlike any other publisher – actual authors that are on the front-lines of what is happening in industry." – Paul A. Sellers, Executive Director, National Sales, Fleet and Remarketing, Hyundai Motor America

"A snapshot of everything you need…" – Charles Koob, Co-Head of Litigation Department, Simpson Thacher & Bartlet

"Everything good books should be - honest, informative, inspiring, and incredibly well-written." – Patti D. Hill, President, BlabberMouth PR

"Great information for both novices and experts." – Patrick Ennis, Partner, ARCH Venture Partners

"A rare peek behind the curtains and into the minds of the industry's best." – Brandon Baum, Partner, Cooley Godward

"Intensely personal, practical advice from seasoned dealmakers." – Mary Ann Jorgenson, Coordinator of Business Practice Area, Squire, Sanders & Dempsey

"Great practical advice and thoughtful insights." – Mark Gruhin, Partner, Schmeltzer, Aptaker & Shepard PC

"Reading about real-world strategies from real working people beats the typical business book hands down." – Andrew Ceccon, Chief Marketing Officer, OnlineBenefits Inc.

"Books of this publisher are syntheses of actual experiences of real-life, hands-on, front-line leaders--no academic or theoretical nonsense here. Comprehensive, tightly organized, yet nonetheless motivational!" – Lac V. Tran, Sr. Vice President, CIO and Associate Dean Rush University Medical Center

"Aspatore is unlike other publishers…books feature cutting-edge information provided by top executives working on the front-line of an industry." – Debra Reisenthel, President and CEO, Novasys Medical Inc.

www.Aspatore.com

Aspatore Books, a Thomson business, is the largest and most exclusive publisher of C-level executives (CEO, CFO, CTO, CMO, partner) from the world's most respected companies and law firms. Aspatore annually publishes a select group of C-level executives from the Global 1,000, top 250 law firms (partners and chairs), and other leading companies of all sizes. C-Level Business Intelligence™, as conceptualized and developed by Aspatore Books, provides professionals of all levels with proven business intelligence from industry insiders—direct and unfiltered insight from those who know it best— as opposed to third-party accounts offered by unknown authors and analysts. Aspatore Books is committed to publishing an innovative line of business and legal books, those which lay forth principles and offer insights that, when employed, can have a direct financial impact on the reader's business objectives, whatever they may be. In essence, Aspatore publishes critical tools—need-to-read as opposed to nice-to-read books—for all business professionals.

Inside the Minds

The critically acclaimed *Inside the Minds* series provides readers of all levels with proven business intelligence from C-level executives (CEO, CFO, CTO, CMO, partner) from the world's most respected companies. Each chapter is comparable to a white paper or essay and is a future-oriented look at where an industry/profession/topic is heading and the most important issues for future success. Each author has been carefully chosen through an exhaustive selection process by the *Inside the Minds* editorial board to write a chapter for this book. *Inside the Minds* was conceived in order to give readers actual insights into the leading minds of business executives worldwide. Because so few books or other publications are actually written by executives in industry, *Inside the Minds* presents an unprecedented look at various industries and professions never before available.

How to Manage a Law Firm Library

Leading Librarians on Providing Effective Services, Managing Costs, and Updating and Maintaining Resources

Mat #40740791

BOOK & ARTICLE IDEA SUBMISSIONS

If you are a C-Level executive, senior lawyer, or venture capitalist interested in submitting a book or article idea to the Aspatore editorial board for review, please email TLR.AspatoreAuthors@thomson.com. Aspatore is especially looking for highly specific ideas that would have a direct financial impact on behalf of a reader. Completed publications can range from 2 to 2,000 pages. Include your book/article idea, biography, and any additional pertinent information.

ISBN 978-0-314-99180-5

For corrections, updates, comments or any other inquiries please email TLR.AspatoreEditorial@thomson.com.

First Printing, 2008
10 9 8 7 6 5 4 3 2 1

CONTENTS

Sarah L. Nichols　　　　　　　　　　　　　　7
Global Director, Research and Information Resources,
Orrick, Herrington & Sutcliffe LLP
ALIGNING LIBRARY SERVICE LINES WITH
BUSINESS STRATEGY

Thomas B. Fleming　　　　　　　　　　　　19
Director of Information Resources Management,
Jeffer Mangels, Butler & Marmaro LLP
ESTABLISHING AND MAINTAINING A LAW FIRM
LIBRARY

Trish Webster　　　　　　　　　　　　　　35
Library Manager, **Honigman Miller Schwartz & Cohn LLP**
AN OVERVIEW OF LAW LIBRARY SERVICES
AND MANAGEMENT BEST PRACTICES

Mariann Sears　　　　　　　　　　　　　　47
Library Manager, **Thompson & Knight LLP**
PROMOTING THE VALUE OF THE LAW FIRM LIBRARY

Amy Easton Bingenheimer　　　　　　　　65
Manager, Knowledge Management, **Quarles & Brady LLP**
CONVERGENCE: INFORMATION, TECHNOLOGY,
AND TRAINING IN TODAY'S LAW FIRM LIBRARY

Christine M. Stouffer　　　　　　　　　　79
Director of Library Services, **Thompson Hine LLP**
SUCCESSFUL LAW LIBRARY SERVICES:
MANAGING THE BALANCE

Mary Lynn Wagner   **103**
Director of Information Resources,
Keating Muething & Klekamp PLL
CHALLENGES FACED IN THE LAW FIRM LIBRARY
IN THE DIGITAL AGE

Appendices   **119**

Aligning Library Service Lines with Business Strategy

Sarah L. Nichols

Global Director, Research and Information Resources

Orrick, Herrington & Sutcliffe LLP

Introduction

Today's law firm library needs to be run as a business, rather than as an overhead service organization, as has historically been the case. Today's law firm library director or head librarian needs to have significant skills in the areas of financial management; branding and marketing; contract negotiation; revenue generation; and staff management, many of which may be new requirements for the role. In addition, digital technology plays a very significant role in today's law firm library, particularly in a global firm where portability of content and 24/7 access to research tools, content, and assistance is critical. Therefore, law firm librarians must have a high level of current and actionable IT literacy.

The key services provided by a law firm library include training (in terms of navigating available internal and external information resources, as well as practical "how to" training); qualifying content; legal and regulatory research; covering knowledge gaps for practices; providing business research and competitive intelligence (CI) expertise; and alerting and current awareness, where practice and client specific content is pushed out to lawyers and staff real time. Services that are most valued by attorneys include assistance with navigating information resources easily and quickly; deep practice knowledge; and targeted content push so that they don't have to spend time finding the exact information they need—they just get dropped off where they need to be. This list of key services has changed a great deal in recent years, with more emphasis on business research and CI skills, and an increased focus on business development.

All of these services, though of critical importance, can be challenging to manage, because attorneys are not necessarily available to sit through training; they do not necessarily want to retrieve their own information from the intranet; and they do not always have time to consult with researchers to specify exactly what targeted information they require.

Therefore, in the years to come, law firm libraries may increasingly focus on content integration to intranets and client extranets. This process involves providing targeted content, customized to "fit" from a variety of providers, and dropping users off exactly where they need to be, with no navigation or search strategy required. Publishers of digital resources are becoming extremely interested in doing tailored projects in collaboration with law firm librarians and IT staff, where they will unbundle their content and offer it up via IP authenticated links that can be placed on the firm's intranet. Ideally, these links will be accessible on practice or client pages and will jump users to a targeted subset of content from the provider, rather than simply taking them to the home page of the research Web site. Sometimes these offerings are referred to as "e-libraries" but often they can be expressed as logo links that populate a research section, for example, on a client page, and jump the user to a detailed company profile or a docket watch, or a newsfeed.

Challenges in Managing a Law Firm Library

The biggest challenges for today's law firm librarian include providing global information coverage for their firm's attorneys, taking into account the differences in how law is practiced country by country (and the availability of resources in developing countries); managing cost of content—and keeping costs per attorney flat as the firm grows; revenue generation, including capturing fee credits when researchers bill out for their time spent doing research on behalf of clients; keeping growth in expenses below projected growth in firm revenue; and standardizing a level of service so that our clients know what they can expect.

It can be especially challenging to manage the library function for a global firm with various practices, attorneys, and other staff distributed across different time zones. There may be different cultural requirements centering on billing out for researcher time; different policies regarding recovering costs of content; differing legal systems and availability of data; and differing information technology (IT) architecture and telecom system sophistication, as well as differing availability of online content. In addition, some practices are more print heavy than others are. For example, tax attorneys frequently need access to codes that were in force many years ago to review decisions based on old tax law; tax codes from many years ago have not been digitized and must be available to them in print. As another example, litigators need to understand what FASB rules were, often many years ago, when lawsuits were originally filed, and those rules have not been digitized. Some practice areas such as intellectual property and corporate are constantly changing, almost in real time, and require a combination of print and digital resources, with digital resources and usage constantly increasing, whereas others are more stable in terms of the resources they require.

Goals in Law Firm Library Management

The chief goals in law firm library management are to deliver the highest quality service by continually improving research services, practices and general content, as well as training and technical support, in the most cost-effective and efficient ways possible, in tandem with the firm's business strategy.

Indeed, we must continually refine and align our service lines, expense management, and revenue-generating techniques with the top-level strategy decided upon by the chairman and executive committee, or risk becoming irrelevant. I believe it is therefore critical that the law firm librarian report up to a C-level executive who has complete and timely knowledge of that top-level strategy, and will share it in real time. Many law firm library directors report to the chief information officer, who can be expected to have thorough knowledge of both the firm's business and financial strategy as well as the plans, goals, and policies regarding IT architecture, which is, of course, critical.

Keeping the law firm library cutting edge and valued is a collaborative effort, involving all the different levels of library staff, and continual communication with important stakeholders including practice attorneys, and other administrative departments such as finance, human resources, IT, conflicts and others. The leading library managers also understand the value of external networking, sharing best practices where they can do so without jeopardizing client confidentiality and encouraging their staff to network and collaborate with their peers. It is also critical to read relevant publications and access experts via professional associations, content providers, and sometimes even clients.

Law Firm Library Staffing Model: Changing Roles

The basic job titles in a law firm library typically include director; manager; project manager; coordinator; research specialist or librarian; tech services librarian or assistant; and library assistant. Often the director is the bureaucrat of the organization and does not tend to be a research practitioner, focusing more on the operational and strategic elements of running the department. Managers often do continue to do research, sometimes only in particular practice areas and are responsible for managing a team of librarians or researchers who directly support the attorneys and other staff at the firm. Coordinators often tend to be solo practitioners in smaller offices whose responsibilities include all the administrative and technical functions as well as research, collection development, local budgeting and so on. Technical services staff take on an ever more sophisticated portfolio of operational and technology related responsibilities that form the backbone of the department. Finally, the assistants are experts in the daily workings of the administrative and clerical functions, including maintenance of physical collections, acquisitions, accounts payable, vendor contacts, and claims.

In a large firm, there may be a firm wide director with direct reports in the distributed locations, or there may be a matrix organization where the local office managers report in to their local office administration, with dotted line accountability to the firm wide director. There may also be regional managers with responsibility for local office staff, and a mix of large teams and solo practitioners, depending on office size. The "best" staffing model is typically determined based on firm culture; on how the firm prefers to manage its operating expenses (for example, a firm wide departmental P&L versus local office ownership of the operating costs for all departments); and on whether there is a C-level executive with an advocacy based attachment and particular interest in the function, to whom the firm wide library director can report.

Essential Law Firm Library Management Skills

Today's law firm manager or librarian must acquire several key skills in order to become successful at managing the law firm library, including budgeting; contract negotiation; project management; IT skills; marketing of services; and personal marketing skills, including demonstrable business savvy and the ability to network.

These skills are increasingly necessary, because the research operation at a law firm needs to be highly visible and considered to the firm's success rather than an overhead drain on resources. Managers need to think of the library function as a business as well as a service, and run it in keeping with that concept from a financial and operational standpoint. They must also continually assess and reassess what their clients need, and deliver it to them. It is also increasingly necessary to call attention to the law firm library's departmental contributions and successes—or risk being perceived as redundant. A variety of methods can be leveraged to publicize the library, including electronic newsletters, regular columns in an internal publication sponsored by the communications department, if your firm has one, vendor hosted training events, research skills sessions that are delivered for CLE credit, and attendance at practice and partner meetings when possible. It is always a good thing to have a library logo and brand identity; the marketing department can often help with this.

Benchmarks to Measure Library Management Success

There are several benchmarks that can be used to measure the effectiveness of law firm library management, including operating expense per lawyer (OEPL) over time; level of influence in terms of client acquisition and expanded relationships with existing clients; cost of content per attorney; staff attrition; return on investment (ROI) on content contracts; and external reputation.

One method used by our 1,100 attorney-firm to measure the department's effectiveness is our annual internal customer satisfaction survey. These surveys, administered by third parties, have been very effective for us, especially when we know the practice area, role, and tenure of the respondents. The following are some of the issue areas that we cover in our annual survey, with numerical ratings from one to five assigned to each response.

- Research support: Overall support provided, including knowledge of content, online resources, and practice/subject areas, as well as timeliness and the quality of the services and end products
- Digital content and online research tools: Comprehensiveness and practice focus of digital content, provided via the portal or through online research platforms

- Print collections: Availability or print resources not covered by digital offerings, either in your local office or in the R&I network
- Overall service: Attitude friendly, respectful, and courteous
- Overall responsiveness: Meets deadlines, takes initiative, adapts to changing requirements as needed
- Overall quality: Error free deliverables; meets or exceeds professional standards
- If the research department/library were a business, how likely are you to recommend its services and products to a colleague?

We also ask for attorney feedback for each individual performance review, annually and at bonus time. This feedback is very relevant in terms of seeing departmental progress, as well as progress for an individual. Based on this feedback, important trends can be picked out, such as knowledge gaps in particular practice areas; whether partners are aware of our service lines; whether print collections are adequate; whether people are comfortable with the training they get, etc. We can then tailor our business strategy around those areas with perceived deficits. In one of our offices, we brought on a large group of lateral hires in a practice area new to that office in the middle of the year, and of course had not budgeted for content to support that practice. We were reminded via the customer satisfaction survey that we needed to significantly enhance the collection available to them, and did so. The different managers have used feedback on individuals to help structure development plans for the coming performance year that addresses any issues isolated via attorney feedback at review time, such as inadequate written communication skills or lack of understanding of resources in a particular practice area.

Evaluating and Implementing New Technologies

When evaluating various new technologies for a law firm library, it is important to consider several criteria:

- Is the proposed technology compatible with existing IT architecture/infrastructure and downstream goals for that architecture?

- Do we have the internal knowledge on the applications engineering team, web engineering team, or networking engineering team to support the proposed technology?
- Can the proposed technology be utilized by other departments in addition to the library or research units?

The cost/benefit and risk/return analysis that is typically applied in this process includes the cost of automating something rather than doing it manually; cost per user; capital expenditure vs. operating expenditure (for example, application service provider (ASP) hosted solutions rather than hosted in-house with server purchases, etc.); and the cost of a multi-year contract with discounts weighed against the need to embrace emerging/improving technologies.

The implementation methods that have proven most effective for new technologies or other specialized or innovative library materials include small user group testing; involving the user community at the beta stage; always having a Plan B and failover steps in place; and publicizing the new technology/materials at every possible juncture, using every possible avenue. The worst mistake you can make is not involving the potential users of an application or product in the trial and testing process.

Preparing for New Technologies

There are several proactive steps that law firm librarians/managers can take in order to prepare for the implementation of upcoming technologies. For example, if you do not report in to the CIO (and especially if you do!), you should do your best to build excellent relationships with key IT department members, and if possible, get an applications engineer and/or web engineer assigned to you, as at least a part of their role. Also, consider that professional development tracks for research specialists and librarians should include a technology focus, rather than only the more "traditional" skill sets of research and training techniques.

Such strategies can assist a law firm library in the integration of new technology, because there is additional internal advocacy and credibility if you have demonstrable IT abilities within or attached to your group. These proactive strategies also enable you to more quickly evaluate new technologies and their fit for your firm; and because of the project management skills resident in the IT organization, you can move to implement the technologies more quickly, bearing best practices in mind.

Everyone in the department should be involved in this proactive process, along with the IT staff—as beta testers, project managers, champions, systems administrators, and data, or content managers. The benefits to legal researchers from being involved in this process include a more varied career path; easier and more efficient/effective ways to do more with less (either with less time or with fewer resources); and credibility as someone who is forward thinking, with cutting-edge skills.

Top Budget Items for Law Firm Libraries: Controlling Costs

The top budget items for most law firm libraries include content; staff; professional development; IT contracts and maintenance agreements; and real estate. IT contracts and maintenance agreements have increased significantly in recent years as we pursue more digital initiatives such as a full automation of our libraries firm wide, and this will remain true in the years to come. Real estate costs will decrease, however, as digitization occurs and we migrate away from print. Financial management techniques that can be used to control costs include enterprise purchasing, where you consolidate separate contracts with the same vendor into one master contract that covers the entire organization; rigorous contract negotiation; and benchmarking to peers via surveys done by entities such as the major accounting firms, specialized consultancies or industry publications. When armed with information about what the cost structures look like at your peer firms, you can work to manage your economics as well or better.

An established law firm may not allocate a certain percentage of its operating budget to library resources. Indeed, our firm does not operate in that way; instead we "compete with ourselves" year on year to minimize percentage increases in operating expenses, and to keep cost per attorney flat and below that of our peer firms. We look at these metrics as a department with staff and other operating expenses included, and then separately; we also look at them as they relate to the firm's entire cost of content for both practices and for the research function. This budget is approved by our COO and CIO.

At my firm, the department bears the expense of general resources that are utilized across practices, and realizes any recoveries of the same, and the expense of practice-specific resources is allocated to those practices and across offices where those practices are housed, proportionally by practice size.

ROI Calculations for a Law Firm Library

Several ROI calculations can be used to determine the value of a law firm library, including fee credits for timekeepers and recoveries for online resources as they offset the full operating expense of the department; cost of time and resources used on business development research as percent of revenue accrued from new business; and percentage growth of operational cost, as compared to percentage growth in firm revenue.

ROI is an important consideration when managing the law firm's library, because if the cost of the operation exceeds the value derived in terms of direct revenue (fee credits) or downstream revenue, C-level management will consider cheaper ways of getting research done such as retaining research contractors on an as-needed basis, or running an intern program using students from local library or other related programs, and potentially downsize/outsource the function.

Outside Experts or Resources

There are numerous types of outside experts or resources that offer regular support services to law firm libraries. For example, library and knowledge management automation platform providers are key partners in terms of assisting research departments to manage and deliver content and services to lawyers via sophisticated, yet easy to use interfaces. Vendors of client and matter validation software also partner with law firm libraries to assist with accurate cost recovery and to provide ease of use across the portfolio of online research tools by allowing single sign on functionality, for example. Major research providers offer support in terms of benchmarking; sharing industry best practices; and customized product development and content integration.

Several of these vendors have adapted to changes in technology in law library management by offering products through Web-based interfaces, providing secure ASP-hosted solutions and supporting multiple platforms. They recognize the need for global law firms to provide multilingual access to resources, and they understand the need to push content by presenting print and electronic resources based on the practice area and the interests of individual lawyers.

One important element in law library management is the increasing importance of being able to track and allocate costs across the firm, by tracking the time and money that is associated with research work, or the ability to evaluate usage statistics of online and print resources for collection management purposes. Automation platform providers offer tools to do this, as do providers of client/matter validation software. These vendors are beginning to offer 24/7 global support and consultation, which bolsters the trend toward delivering more resources online and via remote access.

Final Thoughts

The most important piece of advice that I can offer on managing a law firm library is to always stay aligned with the top-level business strategy of the firm; strive to continually offer and adapt your services in accord with that strategy; and publicize and market those services at every possible opportunity.

Indeed, there is an outdated and negative phrase that is often applied to infrastructure departments at professional services firms: "Justify your existence." I prefer to think of it as "demonstrate your relevance and come as close to being indispensable as you can." We are most relevant when our activities are tied to the strategy of the chief executives at our law firms, and if we cannot demonstrate that relevance, we risk a scenario in which the library or research function withers or becomes diluted. Visionary executives at law firms know that, in the library, they have an incredibly valuable department staffed with experts who can significantly enhance the practice of law. They decide to make an investment in growing and developing the function and they have high expectations. If we meet those expectations, we will remain pivotal and respected, with extremely satisfying roles and career paths.

Sarah L. Nichols, Orrick, Herrington & Sutcliffe's director of research and information resources, leads a firm wide team of research specialists and other information providers who work with lawyers to deliver the best possible research and reference services on behalf of the firm's clients. Since joining in the firm in 2003, Ms. Nichols has focused on enhancing the portfolio of digital content available to attorneys via the portal, developing practice specializations within the research staff, and improving the economic efficiency of the division firm wide. In addition, Ms. Nichols and her team collaborate with staff from marketing and business development, lawyer development, and knowledge management to deliver the tools, training, and competitive intelligence required to support the firm's legal research, CLE, and other professional development initiatives, as well as contribute to client acquisition and retention activities.

Prior to joining Orrick, Ms. Nichols was the director of West Coast Research and Information Services for McKinsey and Company, a major global management consultancy. She has expertise in the areas of strategic planning, operations, and change management for research functions within professional services firms. While at McKinsey, she reengineered the West Coast research and knowledge management operation, and designed the first program for providing client direct access to researchers and information specialists.

Ms. Nichols has a Master's degree in information science with a background in business research and competitive intelligence, having worked primarily in the practice areas of financial services, real estate, and health care. She began her professional career with Keyser Marston Associates, a real estate consultancy, and was an information specialist for several years at McKinsey before moving into the strategic planning and operations arena.

Establishing and Maintaining a Law Firm Library

Thomas B. Fleming

Director of Information Resources Management
Jeffer Mangels, Butler & Marmaro LLP

Introduction

This is intended for the librarian and or the law firm administrator who is starting a law library. There are many excellent resources in the attached bibliography that will provide more in-depth information and resources to learn more about the management of law firm libraries.

The primary goal of the library is to provide for all the information needs of the firm within its budget restraints. The other library goals fall under this primary goal. The library should also be an integral part of the firm's management of information and knowledge management initiatives and projects. When the library director also manages records, conflicts, and calendaring/docketing, they become a more integral part of the firm's overall planning and use of information, and knowledge management.

Virtually any question can be asked of the library staff as long as it does not involve the library staff making a legal opinion. It is interesting to note that increasingly, the library staff is asked to do non-legal research. These non-legal questions run the gamut from what is the cost of purchasing a yacht in China to what is the market penetration of a distiller.

Starting a Law Firm Library

Getting Started - You will need an experienced law librarian or consultant who can transform the firm's information needs and culture into an effective information center to answer these needs. Lawyers and legal researchers expect the law firm library to be the "go to source" for all their information needs. The individual users' expectations can be difficult to meet. When you do the impossible one day, it will become the expected the next day. The following are important factors after you have determined the firm's information needs:

1) Reporting structure - This can be to a library committee, managing partner, library partner, executive director, or another director. It is important to establish this from the onset.
2) Budget - Working with the firm's management, you need to agree on a budget for staff and materials. The basic structure of the budget should

easily show what categories you and the firm's management needs for budgeting and monitoring expenses. Examples are:

    (a) Salaries
    (b) Online and paper resource categorized by practice group, office, new and renewals
    (c) Supplies
    (d) Contracted services and document retrieval, etc.

3) Physical space - With increasing electronic resources, this is less of a concern, but you need to provide space for the printed materials and attorneys to use them. There should also be PC(s) with access to the firm's network and the Internet. Rules of thumb:

    (a) Floor load 150 lbs. to 175 lbs. per square foot or 20 lbs. per linear feet of books, compact shelving 250 lbs. to 300 lbs. per square foot
    (b) Lighting - 75 candle power throughout
    (c) Square footage should be about the same as the linear feet of shelving
    (d) Aisles need to be at least 3" apart (American's With Disabilities Act requirement)
    (e) Study areas - 1 for each 30 attorneys but this is constantly changing
    (f) Work areas for the staff

4) Ordering electronic and paper resources - With an understanding of the firm's culture, you can order the correct mix of electronic and paper resources.

5) Staffing - Based on the number of attorneys, you need to hire the necessary staff. A rule of thumb is about one library staff person to thirty to forty attorneys, assuming you will be contracting out the loose-leaf filing.

6) Catalog and check-in system - Pick a system that matches you needs and budget. Also, make arrangements to catalog the collection at least on a rudimentary basis.

7) User guides - Develop and maintain them ideally on your firm's intranet. These should include the following:

    a) Mission and collection development statements
    b) Services provided - The best way to manage expectations is to say what it is that you can do

c) Library staff - Keep it current with pictures, e-mail addresses, location and telephone numbers

d) Layout of the library - This would show the general layout. Individual titles should also be available via OPAC (Online public access catalog). If you do not have one, you should make the titles available on the firm's intranet.

8) Policies and procedures for the library - Make sure to write down all the internal policies and procedures for the library staff. This will help with cross-training and when there are staff changes.

Library Staff

While you may not have all of the following library staff positions, you need to cover these areas of the library. For smaller libraries, one person would be doing all of these functions.

1. Director/Manager
2. Reference, librarians and or clerks
3. Technical service, librarians and or clerks

The newest variation on the above is to include an "electronic librarian," a person who manages the electronic resources. This person can be either on the library or IS staff. The library director needs to develop and maintain a good working relationship with the IS director because more and more information is now accessed via the Internet or the firm's network. In general, staffing models will vary from firm to firm; the best staffing model is always the one that best manages the firm's information needs and takes advantage of the firm's other staffing resources.

While the majority of the resources are now electronic, they are not exclusively so. All of the library staff must know how to effectively use the information, regardless of the format. They must also stay current. When there is more than one library staff person, each person needs to know how to do the others' jobs. This is when the library's policies and procedures are invaluable. The best way to stay current is to be an active member of the various professional organizations and their respective listservs.

Required Skills

The following (in no exact order) are important skills for library directors and librarians:

1. Research - A good understanding of legal and non-legal research. While you do not have to be an expert, you need to know where to find the answer.

2. Vendors - You should have a good understanding of your primary vendors and how they operate. This enables you to use the services and products to the best advantage and make suggestions for improving them.

3. Financial - You have to be able to manage the financial operations of the library and produce the necessary reports for the budget and monitoring the expenditures. You also need to be able to find ways to improve the service while staying within the budget or even under the budget.

4. Personnel - You need to know how to manage people in all aspects, i.e., hiring, firing, mentoring, managing expectations, improving performance, managing the personnel expenses.

5. Professional development - Stay current by being active with your professional associations. In addition, you need to stay up with new technologies and to determine what will be useful to the users.

6. Branding and Marketing the Library - Be proud of the work that you library does by branding everything that you do. That is done by marking all of the library's work product so that everyone knows that it came from the library. You should also actively market the resources and capabilities of the library.

7. Be the information center of your firm by forwarding items that will be of interest to the management and the practice groups. A good example is to forward the annual surveys (Top 100 and 200 law firms, library, technology, associate satisfaction, etc.) of the *American Lawyer* to the appropriate people.

8. Be flexible - Know how to take on other administrative duties as they are assigned. Having additional departments report to the library allows the library director to better implement new policies and procedures to improve the use of information and knowledge management within the firm.

The following are methods for attaining these skills.

1. The Master's Degree in Library Science (MLIS) is very good because it provides the basic understanding of the profession and the various components. Many programs, classes and even the MLIS programs are available via the Internet.
2. Find a mentor who can help you develop your career and give advice.
3. Become professionally active and attend conferences and programs.
4. Read up on the profession, management, and new technologies.
5. Teach and write articles—teaching and writing are the best way to truly learn a subject.
6. Read about or take courses in management—*Getting Things Done* by David Allen is a great book on how to organize your life and work to obtain what you want. His Web site, http://www.davidco.com/, is also a great resource.

Budgeting

The library director must know how to prepare and manage budgets and monitor expenditures. With the increasing use of electronic information, they must also be able to negotiate contracts and licensing agreements. In addition, they have to be able to predict what will be happening with their major vendors. For example, a librarian needs to be able to forecast what will be the effect on their Lexis and Westlaw contracts as more and more of the court materials are available through Pacer, court sites, and other free or less expensive sources. One last point—establish a policy that all invoices for electronic or paper information have to be approved by the library. When you do this, you usually find many people who are ordering items on their own. The library should be responsible for all the paper and electronic information that is purchased by your firm.

Budget Priorities by Expenditure

The following are the usual Library expenditures ranked by cost:

1. Electronic information
2. Paper information
3. Staff

4. Contract reference

5. Training

A rule of thumb is that 80 percent of the operating budget is allocated to paper and electronic resources. The main consideration when deciding the library's annual budget is trying to meet all the users' wants and needs. Another factor is the amount charged to and received from clients for online research and reference work. You should also track the cost per attorney and per practice group. While there is no rule of thumb on how much to spend per attorney or practice group, tracking it will allow you to predict the cost when the net number of attorneys increases or decreases. Traditionally, the litigation, tax, and corporate practices groups require the most resources of the library. The library must have an effective way to track the use of online and network programs to ensure that they are being used.

Other Considerations

The basic service of the library is responding to the individual information needs of the attorneys. The larger the size of the firm, the larger the expenditures are for the library. Larger firms have certain advantages and can usually negotiate better contract terms for both paper and electronic resources. Larger firms can also afford more specialized staff. With the advent of e-mail and the Internet, it is possible to have specialists in different offices offering services to all of the users, no matter where they are.

Because the attorneys' information needs are the basis of the services that the library provides, each practice area adds its own complexity. There are some practice groups, such as tax and intellectual property, that can be almost totally electronic, while others, such as real estate and government, are more paper-based.

It is now standard to have an automated library program that lists all the information resources that are available through the library. This program should also have the ability to tell when something has not come in. With this ability, the library staff can be alerted when a supplement and/or update has not been received. Additionally, the library staff should be on the lookout for items that are not up to date. Finally, the end users should alert library staff when they come across out-of-date materials. However, this is a last line of defense and should be avoided at all costs. When an out-of-date material is identified by a user, we determine why it was not caught by the library program and correct the process.

The "yell theory" of management is a great way to monitor how the library is performing. As long as no one is yelling, you are all right day to day. If someone is yelling or complaining, the library director should follow up and correct the situation. On a random basis, the requests should be monitored to make sure they are properly dealt with and the requestor is satisfied with the information. On a yearly basis, there should be a user's survey. Any problems, concerns or suggestions should be studied and appropriate action be taken. The library director should implement any changes that are within their purview. The other ones should be discussed with management before implementing them.

Electronic Resources

The fundamental shift in library maintenance has been from the paper to the electronic resources. Initially, the basic information was the same in the electronic format as it was in the paper. Now the electronic version is offering many more features, such as internal links and interactive charts. In addition, the users are asking for customized access to their information such as customizing their portals to RSS feeds and beyond. The library should be prepared to help the users with all of this.

The library should deliver most of the reference work electronically. This enables the requestor to review the information anytime and any place. It has the added benefit of allowing the library staff to keep copies of all the research in case the original is lost and it can become a knowledge management resource. A number of law libraries are also using intranet and/or Wikis as a knowledge management resource.

When managing a library today, it's essential to be very knowledgeable about electronic resources on the firm's network and the Internet. To manage these electronic resources, the library director has to be able to negotiate the contract, monitor the licenses, track the IDs and passwords, report on the usage, and ensure compliance with the copyright laws. In many law firms, it is the library director who oversees the firm's copyright compliance.

How to Implement New Technologies

One of the library director's responsibilities is to monitor new technologies to determine which ones would be useful to the firm. They should always be looking at the ROI (return on investment) value of a new technology. The usefulness of the technology is also a primary concern. The ideas can come from anyone in the firm. The basic criterion is that it has to be useful and better than what is currently available. It is important to find champions within the firm who can help you implement this new technology. Generally, the steps to implement a new technology will look something like:

1. Identified the need
2. Survey available options
3. Present proposal
4. Test
5. Implement
6. Monitor the usage
7. Continually improve

All of these areas can potentially present pitfalls. The effective library director knows how to avoid them. A good philosophy is to ask for forgiveness instead of asking for permission. This enables the library director to try new things that will not greatly disrupt the users.

It is important that you look at a new technology to see all the possibilities it can offer. It also really helps if you can predict who the winners and losers will be. You may not always be right but at least you tried to improve the research capabilities. The worst is to let your resources stagnate.

The primary people to start the implementation process are IS and the library director. If they do not agree on a new technology, it does not go any further. Once they agree, it goes to the executive director, then the library, technology and/or the management committees, depending on the technology. The goal should be to provide the information to the researcher anytime and any place cost effectively.

Implementation Case Study

The following is a personal case study of the implementation of a new technology, the CLE (continuing legal education) from PLI (Practising Law Institute) and an internal password database to track IDs and passwords.

The following are the steps that were involved for each:

PLI's CLE
1. Need - Attorneys kept asking the library for recommendations for CLE programs. While this was not technically under the library, it was an information need expressed by our users.
2. Survey - Obtained recommendations from various online vendors and tested their product.
3. Proposal - Made a proposal to the library committee and then to the management committee and it was approved by both.
4. Test - Created the link on our intranet and tested among a few users to work out any bugs.
5. Implement - Rolled the link out to the attorneys and paralegals and conducted in-house training. Send announcements to the attorneys and paralegals of new offerings and reminders.
6. Monitor the usage to check on active and inactive users. We then randomly check them to see how it is working for them. Produce monthly reports to the library committee on the usage and ROI, both of which have been very good.
7. Improve - Added new features as they appear such as MP3 programs. Monitor other vendors to make sure that our offerings are the most suited to our needs.

Password Database
1. Need - The number of online IDs and passwords were growing unmanageable with many users forgetting their IDs and passwords.
2. Surveyed possible vendors for solutions. The only one that was workable was not worth the investment. The ROI was not acceptable because we could build one in-house for less money.

While it did not have as many features, it provided what we needed.

3. Proposal - Worked with the IS department to work up a proposal to create an in-house database of the IDs and passwords. During the process, we decided to include the attorneys' e-filing IDs from the courts. Presented the plan to the IS, library, and management committees, where it was approved.

4. Test - Developed a beta version that was tested by some users. It was refined based on their input.

5. Implement - The final version was rolled out and announced in a firm wide e-mail.

6. Monitor - Continually monitoring the usage and checking with the users to make sure they know if it available and how to use it.

7. Improve - Developing a Pinpoint Training Video for "Just In Time" Training. These are three to five minute videos on the intranet that show the user how to use a service.

Maintaining a Law Library

There should be a procedure in place to incorporate new ideas and suggestions for improvement. One method is to have weekly meetings of the library staff to go over new ideas and suggestions. If the library staff believe they are worthwhile and they do not have a significant actual or staff cost involved, they are implemented by the library. If they require additional funding, they need to go to the appropriate management person or committee for approval.

Contracting Out

Contracting out of some of the library functions is a good way to improve services without hiring additional staff and or increasing the in-house resources. The most common outsourced functions are the loose-leaf filing and document retrieval. Contracting with a good loose-leaf filing service will ensure that your paper collection is up to date without hiring additional staff. Document retrieval services are the best known types of contracted out reference work. It is impractical for most libraries to send their own staff to retrieve materials from other libraries and courts.

Utilizing Information Audits/Collection Rebalancing

An information audit/collection rebalancing is important both on a macro and a micro level. The macro level should be done yearly during the budget process. The micro level should be done whenever you are viewing a particular area of information or even a particular book. The basic question to consider is what is the most effective and cost-efficient way to make the information available. This varies from the infrequent usage (use an outside provider such as Lexis and Westlaw), to a heavy used source of information where you would purchase an unlimited use license. The goal of an audit should be to ensure that the collection and all its parts are the most cost effective and efficient that they can be. There is a dual benefit to the end user and the bottom line for the firm. The library director is in the best position to conduct an information audit, with management review. Each major vendor is more than willing to do one but they will be biased to their own products. An alternative would be to work with a consultant.

Resources for Staying Current

With constantly evolving technologies, it's crucial for librarians to stay current. The following are some important resources and strategies.

1) Professional associations—these national ones and their local chapters
   a) American Association of Law Librarians (AALL), www.aallnet.org
   b) American Bar Association (ABA), www.abanet.org
   c) ASIS&T - The American Society for Information Science & Technology , www.asis.org
   d) SLA - Special Libraries Association, www.sla.org
2) Listservs and Internet sites
   a) Gene Tyburski's www.thevirtualchase.com
   b) Sabrina Pacifici's www.llrx.com
   c) Internet Lawyer, www.internetlawyer.com
3) Professional meetings
4) Classes - Internet and in person
5) Teach, write, and mentor - It will keep you fresh
6) Read and select your data feeds - Continually read in your librarianship (law and general) profession, management, and technology
7) Consult - It will stretch your mind

Conclusion

In summation, the five focus areas for a law firm librarian or partner responsible for managing the firm's library should be:

1. Information Goals - Managing expectations: Determine what is expected of the library in services and resources and what is the budget. Because these are continually evolving, it is important that it be reviewed at least yearly. Libraries among law firms can vary greatly, the best ones are the ones that meet the needs of its own firm. The library director should be very sensitive to this and create the necessary library for the firm. On the other hand, the library director needs to know other possibilities because the firm and its needs may change.

2. Resources, both electronic and paper - Based on the first focus area, develop the collection to answer the information needs. The right resources and mix of format is also vital and is unique to each firm. You will want to be on the cutting, not bleeding, edge of technologies to keep existing attorneys and attract laterals. Have a way to track the online usage of all your electronic resources.

3. Staffing - Again, based on the first focus area, develop the necessary staff. The staff must be well trained and supervised so they can provide the best service possible within the budgetary restraints.

4. New technologies - Always stay abreast of the new technologies to determine which ones would be useful. As with focus area 2, you have to have the correct technologies to keep and attract attorneys.

5. Integration with the firm - It is important that the library be an integral part of the firm and its technologies, procedures, and culture. The library should integrate smoothly with the firm, especially with technology. You need the technology within the firm to maintain the electronic resources and use it to the best advantage.

Bibliography

General References:

AALL Publications Series, AALL (www.aallnet.org), published by Hein

AALL Spectrum, AALL (www.aallnet.org)

"American Layer's Library Survey," (http://www.americanlawyer.com/) annually

Basics of Law Librarianship by D. Panella, Haworth Press (http://www.haworthpress.com), 1991

Beyond the Boundaries: Report of the Special Committee on the Future of Law Libraries in the Digital Age, AALL (www.aallnet.org), 2002

Briefs in Law Librarianship series, AALL (http://www.aallnet.org/sis/ripssis/briefs.html)

Law Library Information Reports, Glanville Publishers

Law Librarians: Making Information Work, AALL (www.aallnet.org)

    Guide #1 - How to Hire a Law Librarian

    Guide #2 - Expanding Roles of Law Librarians

    Guide #3 - Space Planning for Law Librarians

    Guide #4 - Collection Rebalancing for Law Libraries

    Guide #5 - The Internet as a Legal Research Tool

    Guide #6 - Negotiation in Law Librarians

    Guide #7 - Using the Library as a Marketing Resource

    Guide #8 - Changing Roles of Law Librarians

"Law Librarians and Library Design, Construction, and Renovation: An Annotated Bibliography and Review of Literature" by Thomas R. French, 98 *Law Library Journal* 99-155, 2006

Law Librarianship in the Twenty-First Century, edited by Roy Balleste et al, Scarecrow Press, 2007

Law Library (year) (title varies), Practising Law Institute (www.pli.edu), annual

Law Library Benchmarks, Primary Research Group, Inc, annual (Primarydat@aol.com)

Law Library Journal, AALL

Legal Reference Service Quarterly, Haworth Press (http://www.haworthpress.com)

"Legal Reference Services: An Annotated Bibliography" by Debbie Grey, 97 *Law Library Journal* 537- 564, 2005

Legal Research and Law Library Management by Julius Marke, et al., Law Journal Press, Second Edition, 2008 (loose-leaf)
Salary Survey, AALL (www.aallnet.org), biennially
Survey on Job Descriptions by Patricia Cervenka, Rothman, 1997
Trends in Law Library Management and Technology, Rothman, 1987-

Collection

Directory of Law Related CD-Roms by Arlene Eis, Infosources, annual (?? Get others)
Law Books in Print, Bowker, annual
The Law Library Reference Shelf: Annotated Subject Guide by Elizabeth Matthews, 4th Edition, Hein, 1999
Legal Information Alert, Alert Publications, www.alertpub.com
The Legal Information Buyer's Guide and Reference Manual by Kendall Svengalis, Rhode Island Law Press, biennially
Legal Newsletters in Print by Alrene Eis, Infosources, (annual)
The Legal Researcher's Deskbook, Arlene Eis, Infosources (biennally)
Price Index for Legal Publications, AALL (www.aallnet.org)
Survey on Collection Development Policies and Selection Practices by Vincente Garces, Hein, 2006

Thomas B. Fleming is the director of information resources management for the law firm of Jeffer Mangels Butler & Marmaro LLP in Los Angeles. As such, he is in charge of the library, records, conflicts, and court services (calendaring and docketing). Mr. Fleming has thirty-five years of experience in private and government law libraries and he has written and spoken often on the subject of integration of new technologies into the practice of law. He has also taught at the University of Maryland and Catholic University graduate school of library science in legal research and law library management.

An Overview of Law Library Services and Management Best Practices

Trish Webster

Library Manager

Honigman Miller Schwartz & Cohn LLP

Introduction to Managing a Law Library

The scope of a law library manager's job is continually expanding. Management of digital content is increasingly complicated as vendors produce more content in digital format and present complex and expensive licensing options. The law library is becoming more crucial to business development efforts as the marketing department moves beyond beauty contests, targeted ads, and sponsorships to implement more strategic efforts that are directed at specific clients and industries. The library has a distinct role in these efforts to assess information sources, gather intelligence, and synthesize data into accurate, succinct packages to be used by attorneys and business development team members.

The general goal of our library is to provide high value service to our attorneys and staff.

Specifically, we aim to:

- Deliver accurate research results in a time-sensitive manner.
- Provide regular and effective training on legal research methods, and use of specific resources and tools.
- Maintain a library collection, both physical and online, which enables attorneys to deliver superior legal services to clients.
- Scan the legal services environment regularly for technology developments and provide access to pertinent resources.
- Monitor expenditures and work within budgetary guidelines in providing all of the above.

The firm places an emphasis on high-quality legal service, with a commitment to be creative, pragmatic, and cost effective in delivering this service to clients. The library strives to align itself with this overall objective.

The Library Team

The basic job titles in a law firm library include managers, researchers, and catalogers, among others. Certainly, a firm larger than mine might have a more specific division of labor than we do. The librarians at my firm are all generalists in the sense that we can all take on research assignments from throughout the firm. We work together in deciding on new sources to evaluate and license. One librarian in particular focuses on training initiatives. One maintains the electronic catalog. We all work with the marketing department to provide information on new and existing clients, industries, and competitors. We also do some work with the recruiting committee to help identify lateral candidates.

Two of our librarians are also attorneys and members of our ethics committee. They devote the majority of time to clearing conflicts for new engagements, which involves working closely with our records department as well as legal research of specific conflicts and ethics issues.

Key Library Services

Research, both legal and otherwise, is the main service of the law library. The legal research we provide is still the most valued service by attorneys as it relates directly to their work product. We provide the "raw materials" for the attorneys to do their jobs every day. Our librarians perform substantive legal research and are well versed in the use of a wide variety of sources. The information they provide is synthesized into a concise, understandable package, which in turn allows attorneys to focus on their analysis.

Our non-legal research is also highly valued, particularly when it involves finding information that an attorney suspects is "on the Web," but does not have the first inkling about where to start looking for it. We are very familiar with specialized databases and their search techniques, government sources of information, sources for statistics and economic research, and much more. This non-legal research encompasses a larger proportion of our requests than it has in the past. This is partly due, I think, to the huge increase in content on the Web. Our users seem to become overwhelmed more quickly, and thus turn to the library for help more often. It is also due in part to the fact that we have been building a stronger relationship with our marketing department, which means they come to us for research help more often—whether on prospective clients, a specific industry, or our competitors.

Training, in the use of a variety of online materials, as well as traditional print legal materials, is another important service. Our firm supports legal research training for summer and new associates, but there never seems to be quite enough time dedicated to it, given the obvious need. It is also a constant challenge to get attorneys to optional training sessions, whether on a specific online product or a specific legal topic. We tend to try to take advantage of opportunities to do some training "on the fly" when an attorney has a specific need that allows us to focus on a resource or topic.

Finally, the law library also provides content management, through alerts, specialized news and legal products, feeds, etc. Content management for our end users presents unique challenges, since it seems as if the sources of information increase so rapidly. We strive to evaluate new sources as they are brought to our attention, but obviously, we cannot do an in-depth evaluation of everything that comes our way. Since we prioritize time-sensitive client work, content management issues are often moved to the bottom of the list, and it's not always possible to dedicate as much time as we would like to these issues. Much of what has proven to be useful in the area of content management has required a bit of trial and error. For example, we created a daily newsletter on a company that was being targeted for new business development. The newsletter was produced in the library and sent daily to the individuals on the client development team. While a small number of attorneys praised the newsletter, some more detailed follow-up in the form of a survey revealed that a majority of the team was deleting the e-mails without even reading them. In light of the fact that the newsletter was very time consuming to produce, we significantly scaled back its production. It is important when trying new ideas not to wed yourself to closely to the first (or second, or third) iterations of the idea and to be willing to tweak it in light of user feedback so that everyone's time is being used as effectively as possible.

Necessary Skills for Managers

Law libraries often seem to function on their own in some ways, apart from other law firm administrative departments who often are not quite sure what the library does. I see that changing as teamwork becomes more common as other departments, such as marketing, accounting, and human resources, are asking the library to support their efforts and their individual information management needs. Managers should be willing to work with other departments, and should make regular efforts to communicate with other department heads in order to find out ways that the library can assist them in meeting the needs of the firm. They should make an effort to be outgoing, and cultivate networks throughout the firm.

Law library managers must be adept at research themselves, as an understanding of the process is key to understanding the needs of clients (library clients, not firm clients).

Managers should be good communicators, and cultivate an understanding of people from diverse backgrounds, so that they are able to work successfully with attorneys, library staff, and people from other departments within the firm. Along with this, they should be able to work well in teams, as there is an increasing need for library staff to work with teams throughout the firm to help with their information management needs.

Managers need to be curious about information science, the legal field, business administration, and technology. They should use this curiosity to spur them to regularly monitor developments in these fields, and take action when needed to investigate new resources, alert constituents to important developments, and initiate changes to practices and processes when warranted.

Becoming a good researcher happens over time through a combination of training and doing. Training is available in traditional library science and legal classes, through library and competitive associations, and frequently from vendors of specific research sources. The doing part happens over time as any law firm research position will present an unpredictable array of research assignments.

While some communication skills are innate or learned earlier in one's career, regular effort needs to be made to exercise and update skills such as writing and public speaking. Attention should also be paid to more informal communications. Library managers should avail themselves of opportunities to participate in department meetings and regularly talk to our customers about their experiences with the library. Teamwork can be developed within the library itself or by getting involved with initiatives that work across departments. Opportunities at my firm have come up in the form of evaluating new document management providers, a documents retention policy committee, and a Web site development committee.

Negotiation skills are important for managing content, both print and digital. It's also important to communicate with internal clients (library users) to accurately access their information needs so that resources (money and staff time) are being used most effectively to support their true needs.

The ability to juggle multiple assignments and stay cool under pressure is more important than ever as the library receives an ever higher volume of requests from the simple to the complex.

Finally, to keep abreast of developments in information science, legal services, business, and technology, one should monitor Web sites of associations and legal blogs; scan news on these topics in newspapers, journals, and magazines; create alerts on specific topics, clients, or industries; and attend conferences or workshops to develop specific skills and learn about new technologies and best practices.

Managing New Technologies

Digital technology is simply a huge area for us. As the amount of information available digitally grows at a phenomenal pace, the library is charged with helping to make sense of it all for users. We have the skills needed to determine the authoritativeness of sources, evaluate user interfaces, and determine which are most effective for users. We are continually acting as filters to try to make sure that what gets delivered to attorneys and other clients is the best and most pertinent information, reducing the amount of less relevant or outright useless digital noise in our users' information environment.

Evaluating New Technologies

When considering a new technology, we don't do a formal cost/benefit and risk/return analysis, but rather, look at the overall picture of how updating a technology or adding a new one aligns with the core service objective of the library. It often involves a weighing of the expense and time involved in a new initiative against what we are currently doing to fulfill the need. For example, in the case of RSS feeds, we have determined that one of the best things we can do right now is have librarians acting as gatekeepers for RSS feeds, and sending along only the most substantive clips to individual attorneys, client teams, or marketing personnel. We looked at licensing an aggregator firm wide, but decided that at this time the demand for technology to monitor specific clients and topics is being effectively served through "watches" we've set up through Lexis, Westlaw, and some of our other content providers. No doubt we will be addressing this again in the future as the technology evolves.

Similar to the way we make ourselves aware of new technologies, much of this is an informal process. If the technology is relatively inexpensive or free (such as RSS feeds, mentioned above), one librarian will take the lead in "test driving" the technology, then we will meet to discuss and decide whether it is something we want to adopt on a broader scale, considering not only costs in dollars, but also in terms of time requirements of the library staff, and eventually of users.

For something more costly, such as a new service from a vendor, we usually meet after some preliminary information gathering and decide whether the need that the technology fulfills makes it worth the time required for a trial period and/or a vendor presentation. This is when we decide whether the library can evaluate on its own, or whether attorneys should be included as well. While trials are a great way to get feedback from the end users, I have to be particularly sensitive to the time pressures of attorneys and not squander their goodwill by constantly asking them to assist in evaluating products. Once a trial is concluded, participant feedback is gathered either through e-mail or in person and a decision is made whether to adopt the technology or product.

Challenges and Obstacles

Time management is a big issue for the library team. With the high priority we place on the provision of research services, it is increasingly hard to do the background work that allows us to keep up with what is coming next. We are often victims of our own success, in that delivering high-quality responses to research requests creates more requests, whether from the same individuals, or others who hear about our capabilities through the firm grapevine. We have an obligation to keep current with information science trends, technology developments and enhancements, and legal services trends and products. It seems like these tasks could eat up most of a workweek, so you have to pick your battles and not let yourself get buried in the deluge of information that seems to be constantly coming at you.

Managing costs for electronic subscriptions, particularly Lexis and Westlaw, is a constant challenge. As more clients are refusing to pay for electronic research, the firm has to pay a larger proportion of these contracts as overhead. It also is difficult to determine who is using electronic services that have enterprise-wide licenses that don't provide easy access to usage data. Negotiating contracts is always difficult for these services, especially since how vendors price these products is usually a mysterious and/or tortuous process.

Library Size

Our firm has been growing at a moderate pace since I began working here almost nine years ago. Since that time, we have added approximately seventy attorneys and two new offices. I think of this growth as substantial, though not explosive, and it has had some impact on the library, particularly regarding research requests. We have added one librarian position, to help handle the increased research requests.

Firm size does impact content management issues in some ways, since there are additional users to consider when negotiating licenses, whether priced per user or by department or firm size (increasingly common in my experience). Since I monitor Lexis and Westlaw usage very closely, the growth in firm size has meant there's more usage to monitor, and seemingly more occasions when I need to communicate with users about the need to be cost conscious when using these tools.

Practice Areas

Research requests and content management needs vary widely by practice groups. Obviously, litigators tend to present us with the most time sensitive requests, and some of the most complex requests. Transactional practice groups tend to have fewer research requests, although when they do they often are highly specialized in nature, and require the use of specialized resources for economic data or precedent hunting. Tax practice groups still collect many print resources and need a lot of attention to collection updating and weeding, when space becomes an issue.

Measuring the Library's Effectiveness

The library's benchmarks for success and measures of effectiveness are primarily anecdotal. While I collect statistics on requests fulfilled, and monitor expenditures closely to ensure we're meeting budgetary goals, the primary method for monitoring library performance is through day-to-day involvement with staff. The fact that all the library staff is in one office makes it fairly easy to have regular conversations about our performance. I ask for regular updates on progress with research requests, and the librarians meet regularly to discuss new sources, cost-effective use of sources in our collections, and other issues as they arise. I encourage the librarians and staff to keep a "highlights" file on their work that features stellar work product and feedback from attorneys and staff that they serve.

I intend this year to license a product that will allow us to track usage of all our online licenses so that we can determine if we are getting the most out of these products and whether there are some we should be eliminating or renegotiating licenses for.

Additionally, we regularly survey summer associates and new associates as follow-up to research and orientation sessions, and can use this feedback to make changes to future sessions. Survey feedback helps us determine areas where more explanation is needed.

As far as the effectiveness of the library at legal research, we ask for (and receive) regular feedback from attorneys over the course of the assignment. More complex assignments often call for a couple/few conversations with the assigning attorney as the research is developed to make sure that the questions are properly understood and that the research is responsive to the attorney's needs.

The librarians have regular conversations about assignments and opportunities to brainstorm about which sources are most helpful and what approach should be tried to most effectively fulfill requests.

Among the librarians, we all have a responsibility to update our technology and research practices. This is accomplished through regular scanning of magazines, newsletters, blogs, and Web sites. While we focus some of these efforts on sources directed at special or law librarians, we also scan sources directed at attorneys and other firm managers, as well as industry-specific sources that our clients are using. Since there are three librarians in the same office, we take advantage of ad hoc opportunities to discuss new sources and best practices. If we adopt a new technology or practice, we often have a meeting where one librarian takes the lead in training the others. This process is pretty informal since our staff is small. One of our librarians has a background as a Lexis trainer and tends to take the lead in these instances, though any librarian has opportunities to do so.

Budgeting

The top five budget items for law firm libraries are:

- Salaries
- Print collection new purchases and subscriptions/updating
- Lexis and Westlaw
- Other online subscriptions

Our print collection expenses have been decreasing slightly as we move toward more electronic sources and simply reduce the size of the physical collection. The large increase in other electronic subscriptions tends to be larger than the reduction in print spending. One reason for that is that vendors increasingly are offering only enterprise-wide pricing, which tend to be very expensive. At the same time, there is more demand from practice groups and marketing that we provide access to online sources for business and financial data, deal and forms databases, and specialized topical sources offered by expert individuals and firms.

Conducting careful evaluation of new sources before licensing can control costs, as can getting as much user feedback and usage statistics as possible when negotiating licenses. Additionally, developing fair policies to bill use to clients, where appropriate, and communicating the policies and practices consistently to firm users can also cut costs.

Using Outside Experts and Resources

Associations such as SLA, AALL, and SCIP are great resources, along with local chapters of the same. Some of our vendors offer strong support to libraries. Associations offer networking opportunities to interact with other firm librarians who can often offer advice on challenges facing law library managers. Newsletters or journals can be helpful. Conferences and online learning opportunities on specific topics help one keep on top of developments and best practices. Vendors frequently offer training opportunities for their products, whether live, by phone, or online. Account representatives from West and Lexis, along with staff dedicated library relations, can often help raise issues of concern to the right people within these very large organizations.

Conclusion

It seems to me that organizing and accessing the firm's internal information is going to be a challenge that the library might help address in the future. The size of our firm, with offices in only one state, has made it fairly easy for departments (whether administrative or practice groups) to develop their own "information silos," where information can include documents and other work-product, client contact information and intelligence, deal descriptions and data, financial and billing data, and more. As the firm grows and continues efforts to market across departments, it will be more important to find ways to effectively access and analyze data from all these sources.

In conclusion, I would advise library managers not to let perfect be the enemy of good. Managing a law firm library in the current legal environment means facing constant deluge of requests from attorneys and staff, information on current products and practices, vendor solicitations by every means available to them (e-mail, phone, fax, snail mail, dog and pony shows, etc.), internal pressures to lower costs, and requests to add more and better resources all the time (while minimizing overhead expenses, of course). You have to guard against the desire to make everything absolutely perfect before you send it off to an attorney or roll it out to the firm, or else you will be paralyzed. Particularly when trying new things (a product, an open house, a newsletter, an intranet expansion), you have to be willing to accept a certain risk of failure or you will not move forward.

Trish Webster has been a librarian at Honigman Miller Schwartz & Cohn LLP since 1999, and has been the library manager since 2005. She has her Master's in library and information science from Wayne State University, and a Bachelor's degree from John Carroll University.

Promoting the Value of the Law Firm Library

Mariann Sears

Library Manager

Thompson & Knight LLP

Introduction: Services of the Law Library

Above all else, the law library provides requestors with the information they seek in the most economically efficient manner possible. Attorneys value the law library's ability to find what they need quickly and economically because, ultimately, that is what their clients pay them to do. Our goal is to serve our attorneys as best we can so that they can serve their clients as best they can. We serve at the behest and whim of our attorneys, who serve at the behest and whim of their clients, who are our ultimate clients.

The information professionals in our law library also provide the client services department with the business and recruiting information it requires, sometimes analyzing our findings for them. We assist other administrative departments with their information needs as well. We maintain the library's physical and electronic collections, weeding when necessary and making new acquisitions when necessary. We negotiate the purchase and renewal of the library's online contracts, working out the best possible deals for our firms, although this is sometimes difficult because of the confidentiality agreements most vendors require. In addition, we monitor the firm's compliance with numerous licensing agreements, and we sometimes monitor copyright compliance, although attorneys, not information professionals, are perhaps best suited for this role.

While the management of online resources and all that it entails is not a "new" addition to the list of services library managers provide, the explosion in the sheer number of online resources managers must keep track of is a relatively new phenomenon. As a result, library managers are forced to think and behave more and more like business people in their dealings with those who control access to the information we need. Library managers need to know how to read contracts. We need to learn how to negotiate better contracts. Library managers also should be more involved in educating attorneys and firm management about cost recovery issues. Too often, the cost of too much electronic research is absorbed by the firm. If it has not already done so, firm management, with the assistance of library managers, must come to grips with how it will tackle cost recovery, inform attorneys of their philosophy, and work toward accomplishing a solution.

In many firms, including my own, professional librarians charge for the time they spend researching both client-chargeable and firm-chargeable matters. Sometimes, but not often, the client services department informs the library when the research we perform for them has assisted in garnering new business for the firm. Professional librarians at my firm do not have targets for billable hours, but they are encouraged to bill what they can. They perform a significant amount of firm-chargeable research for business development and client services, and this time is included in the timekeeping reports I send to management. They also spend a significant amount of time performing administrative duties—so called "back-end" library work. Some library managers require their professional library staff to track this time as well, but, so far, I have resisted requiring my professional staff to track this time. None of the other professionals in other departments, accounting and IT, for example, are required to track this time to show their worth to the firm, and I remain unconvinced that it is important for professional librarians to track this time to show their worth to the firm.

How New Technologies Have Changed the Way Law Libraries are Managed

The move to Web-based and digital technologies in libraries over the last decade or so has forced library managers to become more involved with the purveyors of those technologies. Our relationships with vendors have changed from telling them what we want to purchase to choosing from among the myriad of products they offer us. Sometimes we contend with hard marketing tactics some vendors have adopted. It seems that everyone has a new digital product to sell us, and some come with unreasonable or unrealistic licensing agreements. In addition, many law firm libraries are shrinking to ridiculously small sizes because there is a misconception that "everything is available online, after all." Of course, library managers know that nothing could be further from the truth. Nonetheless, we are bombarded with this misconception by both vendors and firm management, whom we continually try to educate otherwise. Our physical space is being reduced and reconfigured because firm management often does not view the services we provide as valuable as the dollars they currently spend in square footage for larger, showcase libraries. The "show" in many law firms seems to have shifted from displaying knowledge, i.e., classic libraries with wooden stacks full of books, to displaying technological know-how, i.e., state-of-the-art conference centers filled with cutting-edge technology and expensive artwork. There seems to have been an ideological shift by firm management in this area over the last ten or fifteen years.

Digital technology is both a boon to and the bane of our existence. After all, where would any of us be without e-mail and the Internet? On the other hand, library managers and the attorneys they serve are suffering from a severe case of information overload. There are so many new digital products available to choose from that library managers hardly know where to begin looking for them or how to begin evaluating them. The world is witnessing the beginnings of a technology revolution. Much like the industrial revolution that began about a century ago, the technology revolution will forever change our lives. It will take some time for the revolution to evolve from its current chaotic first phase. One of the responsibilities of library managers is to guide their firms successfully through this first phase, helping firm management separate fact from fantasy, and being always mindful that everything new is built on past foundations.

Acquiring New Technologies

Many library managers will ask a vendor representative to demonstrate a new product or technology. At my firm, the demonstration usually starts with the library manager, and if the product is promising, the library manager will request the vendor to demonstrate it to the entire library staff. If the product has application beyond the library, others also may be invited to the demonstration.

We ask questions like these: Is there a need for this product? Who will benefit from this product? Who will use the product? How much does it cost per user? What results or financial gain, if any, can we expect from the use of the product? What other firms use this product? How easy is it to use? How easy is it to maintain? Do we already have similar products that perform similar functions? How reputable is the vendor? Will the library or the firm acquire a competitive edge if we purchase this product? Will the product eventually pay for itself in new business or in the maintenance of current business?

Sometimes, a partner will tell the library manager that a new product is a "must-have" for his or her practice group. If a library committee member or practice area leader agrees with the partner and approves the purchase request, the library will purchase the product, often without performing a cost/benefit or risk/return analysis. Many times, partners will request that a particular product be purchased just because a competing law firm has purchased that product. Occasionally, after purchasing a particularly expensive resource for a practice area, a member of the practice group will inform the library manager that the resource was used successfully on behalf of an existing client or a new client.

Implementing New Technologies

Some steps I have taken as library manager to implement a new technology include advertising the existence of the new technology or material; inviting potential users to hands-on training sessions and demonstrations; reminding those users of the dates and times for the training sessions; conducting the training sessions; and following up with the users after training to answer questions not posed or thought of during training.

Of course, the biggest pitfall to the implementation of the new technology is getting potential users to attend the training sessions. Offering training sessions during the lunch hour and providing lunch for the attendees, offering many choices for training times, offering training sessions that take no more than thirty minutes, and offering opportunities for one-on-one training or "just in time" training are some of the strategies I have successfully employed in the past to ensure attendance at training sessions.

To educate myself about new technologies and to prepare myself for their implementation, I review technology literature, attend technology conferences, attend library professional development programs, and discuss technology with our IT department. Taking these steps helps ensure the library manager's awareness of new technologies and their possible application to the firm's business. Keeping abreast of new technologies allows the library manager to become a key player involved in the technology decision-making process. Firm management has the final say, of course, on whether the new technology will be implemented. Nevertheless, IT personnel and library personnel can act as advocates for new technologies. Our analysis of the costs and benefits and risks and rewards of the new technology can assist management in the decision-making process.

Library managers should learn all they can about *relevant* emerging technologies. They should be patient about recommending implementation—there is a difference between cutting edge and bleeding edge. They should communicate their knowledge to firm management if necessary, and be prepared to show a cost-benefit analysis. For example, the library at my firm recently purchased a new online current awareness tool for the corporate and securities department. The purchase resulted in the acquisition of a new client who brought the firm revenue that was four times the cost of the new product. The client continues to bring the firm revenue and has more than paid for the cost of the new technology. None of this would have transpired if the library manager had not been made aware of the new technology by reviewing the legal technology literature.

Training Attorneys and Other Users

More and more, I find that my department is called upon to train both attorneys and staff in the use of electronic library resources. Training is most frequently initiated on demand and on a one-on-one basis, rather than in a formal classroom setting. We help attorneys who call us or seek us out navigate and understand new technologies and electronic resources. Unfortunately, many associates do not understand that legal research is an integrated process, and that sometimes, print resources are the more appropriate tools to consult over electronic resources. Because of the generational differences in learning styles at my firm, I am exploring the possibility of training younger attorneys using Webcasts and podcasts.

Regardless of the generation an attorney or other user belongs to, I have found that training sessions in general are smaller, shorter, and more interactive than they have been in the past. Without a doubt, hands-on, live training is the most effective way to update both attorneys and staff on new technologies and research practices. As an example, my department recently introduced a new library maintenance software program. The developer provided extensive live training for the entire staff, which was supplemented by more customized training that a member of my staff developed in-house. Most of the last annual departmental retreat was dedicated to training the staff on the cataloging module of the program. This year we will implement the serials module of the program. The acquisitions and budget modules will be the last ones implemented. All of our training for the new software took place in a live, hands-on environment where the trainees felt comfortable interacting with the trainer.

The Library Team

The library team at my firm includes me, the manager/director, a branch supervisor, four research librarians, some of whom also are competitive intelligence librarians, two non-professional library clerks, and library filers who are hired as independent contractors. Variations on this model abound, however—everything depends on the culture of the particular firm. What works in one place often does not work in another. For instance, some law firm libraries have professional acquisitions librarians, technical services librarians, budget librarians, non-professional librarian assistants, and library administrative assistants.

Regardless of title or position, library staff members are being asked to do more with less. The non-professional staff at many law firm libraries has been shrinking, but the work they do for firm librarians has not gone away. Now, professional librarians pick up much of the administrative slack. Despite the "double duty" we are required to perform because of our shrinking staff, firm management still asks us to show our worth to the firm. It is difficult to show value, however, when there is no room for library staff growth and professional librarians must make time for "back-end" clerical duties as well as their professional duties. It is a bit of a Catch-22 for us.

Necessary Skills for Managers

Negotiation skills are required now more than ever. Business acumen also is a necessity, as we see our firms being managed and run more and more "like businesses." The quest for greater profits seems to outweigh providing excellence in client service at many law firms. Law firm libraries are caught in this quest. We are asked much more frequently to contribute more to profitability and less to firm overhead. Accordingly, tact and diplomacy also are in high demand as library managers communicate with and try to educate firm management about the dynamics of providing information and access to information to the attorneys and other researchers in the firm and the value knowledge professionals can offer to the firm and its members.

Communications skills, both oral and written, attention to detail, adaptability, open-mindedness, patience, knowledge of the firm's business, knowledge of the business of law firms generally, listening skills, knowledge of trends in law librarianship, and decisiveness all should be in a law library manager's skills arsenal. Without these skills, the library manager is merely maintaining the status quo. Without them, the law library manager is not forward-thinking and cannot be a change agent for the firm he or she serves. The skills enumerated above are acquired through experience, professional development programs, experience, self-reflection, experience, discussions with other library managers, and experience. Oh, and did I mention experience?

Maintaining an Up-to-Date Library

Nuts and Bolts

Many library departments, including my own, use a combination of filing services and library staff to update our libraries. Most libraries of any size have library management software that allows them to monitor the receipt of updates and supplements, so that they are continuously aware of what they should have in their libraries at any given time to remain current.

In my department, we check in supplements and updates as they are received, noting whether the previous supplement or update was received and taking appropriate action with the publisher if it was not. We organize the supplements and updates to make it easier for the filing service to locate materials that require updating. The filing service or non-professional library staff locates the materials and files the updates. If we receive updates for materials that cannot be located, we request our attorneys and staff to check in their work areas for the materials. We also "sweep" the office occasionally, looking for missing materials. We update those materials that we locate after our request to the attorneys and the staff or after our office "sweep." If materials remain missing for more than a couple of months, we consider them lost and order replacement copies.

Professional Development Programs

Staff professional development programs are a necessity for a thriving law library, and I am a staunch advocate of my staff's attendance at professional development programs. I have instituted a monthly brown bag WebEx session sponsored by one of our vendors to help my staff and me keep up to date with the latest research practices and technologies. I encourage my staff to attend local, regional, and national library conferences so that they can stay current on what is happening with technology and research practices. We subscribe to and circulate several newsletters and other current awareness materials that inform us of the latest trends and nuances in our field. Fortunately, firm management supports my department's professional development objectives.

Utilizing Outside Experts

The librarian relations managers and consultants at Westlaw and Lexis are a huge support to my firm's library. The Houston Area Law Librarians, the American Association of Law Libraries (AALL) local chapter, is also a great support. The national organizations that support law libraries, AALL and the Special Libraries Association (SLA), also are very helpful. These organizations let my staff and me know what's new in the law library world and offer to train us on new resources and technologies. They let me and my staff know how other law firms have addressed the problems my department currently faces. They reinforce my worth in the large scheme of the law firm. Additionally, they do a better job at predicting and making preparations for upcoming changes in the industry than we do. They do an excellent job at communicating those changes to us and letting us know how they will affect us. Typically, it costs less than $2,000 a year for one person to attend both the AALL conference and the SLA conference. Attendance at programs sponsored by local or regional associations and by vendor alliances come with little or no cost. The connections that are made with other library professionals at these functions are priceless, however. There's nothing better than discussing a particularly thorny issue that is plaguing your department with another librarian who has already dealt with the issue in his or her library.

Budgeting

Where the Money Goes

For an established law firm like mine, generally 1 to 3 percent of the operating budget is allocated to library resources. Naturally, larger firms have larger operating budgets. As a result, library resources may be allocated a smaller percentage of that large operating budget. The total spend may be very large, but the percentage of the overall budget may be insignificant. At my firm, I have noticed a trend developing where the transactional departments (corporate and securities, real estate, energy) are requesting and spending more of the library budget over the last few years. I believe this is because the practice of law has been moving away from the courtroom and more into the boardroom over the last decade or so.

Online services, upkeep of print resources owned by the library, current awareness resources (both print and electronic) for the firm, new print resources, and "desk copies" for the attorneys are the top items in the law library's budget at my firm. Desk copies are portable pamphlet versions of rules and codes that attorneys keep in their offices for ready reference and to take to court or client meetings. By far, the cost of online resources accounts for the majority of the library's budget, and those costs continue to increase at a rapid rate.

The cost of keeping up already owned print resources continues to rise as library managers deal with fewer and fewer legal publishers, but I foresee the cancellation of more and more print resources in favor of electronic resources, so eventually the cost of upkeep for them will decline as we move toward a more digital collection. I definitely am spending less on new print resources. I have also witnessed an explosion in the number of electronic current awareness services in the legal marketplace, and many of those services are excellent and timely additions to our collections. They are often very expensive, however, and licensing agreements can be less than favorable to law firms. The country's copyright laws have not yet come to grips with how the new formats should be handled, and as a result, many libraries will not be able to afford some of the new and valuable resources that come with restrictive licensing terms.

Strategies for Control

Acquiring skills in negotiation with vendors must become part of every library manager's financial management arsenal. Keeping a closer eye on what is used in the collection and canceling resources that are not used often are other strategies that can be employed to control the budget. Like most law firm libraries, my library borrows a good deal from other larger law firm libraries and from the academic law libraries in our area. These libraries are taking the same cost-cutting measures we are, so we may see this budget control strategy come to an end in the future. Indeed, there may come a time when a needed resource can no longer be located in an efficient manner. Finally, a well thought-out library maintenance agreement can help protect against future price increases for the upkeep of print materials that are already owned by the library. Many firm libraries have entered into this type of agreement. As far as I am aware, however, only one legal publishing company encourages participation in such a plan.

Allocation of Library Resources among Practice Areas

Although the allocation will vary from firm to firm, depending on the firm's areas of expertise, at my firm, 40 percent of library resources typically will go to trial resources—cases, statutes, treatises, encyclopedias, digests. Thirty-five percent will go to transactional resources for corporate and securities, tax, real estate, energy; 25 percent will go to specialty areas like IP, international, bankruptcy, and reference.

The percentage of resources marked for federal practice versus state law practice depends on the focus of the firm's practice. Since my firm is more of a regional firm, we focus more on state materials. Other firms have a national focus or focus on regulatory work. As a result, these firms' collections may contain more federal law resources than state law resources.

Challenges for Library Managers

Educating the Folks at C-Level

One of the biggest challenges we library managers have is communicating our value to the organization's management. Firm management often does not know what we do and believes that the library is a huge cost center. Even though this mindset may be due largely to the failure of library managers to educate management in this area, it is difficult to show management that, although the department is expensive to run, the value we provide to the attorneys in particular and to the firm in general is immeasurable. Another related challenge is keeping the cost of maintaining the library at a reasonable level. In terms of costs, library managers often are at the mercy of the legal publishing industry, and the industry itself has fewer and fewer players in it. Additionally, the larger the firm, the greater the distance between the library manager and firm management, which allows for fewer opportunities for the two parties to meet and exchange ideas, philosophies, and information.

Multi-Location Challenges

There are also challenges associated with managing professional and clerical staff across multiple locations. Library managers, including myself, are not always aware of the personal dynamics in other offices. A good and trusted supervisor is key to staying informed about the concerns and accomplishments of the staff in another location. Isolation can sometimes be a factor in an office where there is a single professional librarian. Inclusion in departmental meetings and decisions helps in this area. The key is good communication among all staff members, regardless of whether the communication is virtual or face to face.

Vendor Relations

One of the most difficult services for a library manager to manage is the maintenance and negotiation of our online contracts, which have become more complicated over time, making it difficult to have one contract serve the needs of all the practice groups in the firm.

In most law firms, a few practice areas (e.g., litigation, intellectual property, corporate and securities) are more resource intensive than others are. These practice groups often request that information be provided to them in an electronic format, and sometimes they request that the information be presented in both a print and an electronic format. This can present a challenge because vendors often price electronic resources on the size of the firm as a whole and not on the number of actual users who will require access. Thus, library managers often end up paying for firm-wide user licenses when only a fraction of those licenses are necessary.

Customer Satisfaction

Lawyers and legal researches expect librarians to deliver accurate, current, and timely responses to their research needs. Most lawyers and legal researchers do not understand the cost-effective aspect of library management—they just want their answers. Sometimes it is difficult to offer accurate information in the timeframe the attorneys demand. Their expectations often are unreasonable, considering the scope of their requests. It is always a good idea for library managers to develop a customer satisfaction survey to measure how attorneys perceive them and their effectiveness.

I, like many library managers, request feedback annually from attorneys about the library staff's performance. I am fortunate to receive many responses to my annual inquiry. I receive compliments from attorneys about the effectiveness of my professional librarians' research skills. The feedback I receive is included in the librarians' annual employee review. Of course, there is room for improvement in the implementation of my survey. For instance, I could send a follow-up survey to attorneys with particularly difficult or involved information needs and ask specific questions about how the library research staff met the attorney's needs. One question I should definitely ask is whether the library's assistance was beneficial to the attorney's client and whether the librarian's responses assisted the attorney in "closing the deal." Feedback indicating that there was some financial gain or goodwill received from the client is the best indicator of the library's return on the firm's investment.

Conclusion

Law library managers should not be afraid to let the C-level managers know the value their department has to the firm. They must toot their own horns, because no one else will do it for them. All too often, the department is viewed only as a cost center and not as a potential profit source. Library managers must continue to do what it takes to change this perception.

In summation, library managers might focus on the following five areas to improve their departments and their service to the attorneys who comprise their firms:

1. Always strive to provide timely, accurate, and current information to the attorneys and others who request it by using the most cost-effective and efficient resources available. This is the raison d'être for our existence in law firms. Attorneys need timely, accurate, and current information to advise their clients. Without it, they will not retain clients and cannot hope to obtain additional clients. Timely, accurate, and current information imparted to clients is the cornerstone of a successful law firm's existence. In reality, it is the cornerstone of the existence of any successful business. Qualified information professionals who know how to find and use the appropriate resources available to them in the most cost-efficient manner is one of the keys to success in accomplishing this goal. Of course, law firms should provide librarians with sufficient resources that will allow them the opportunity to use their professional skills to the firm's advantage.

2. Strive to keep control of your budget by being vigilant about the composition of your collection. Law firms cannot spend an unlimited amount of money on resources, so the library manager must have the knowledge and experience to choose wisely among the services offered. The less firms spend on so-called "overhead" items like library resources, the more profits partners can put into their pockets. Knowledgeable and experienced library managers who can work with and negotiate with vendors for the best possible price for the information resources their firms require and who can communicate their negotiation successes to firm

management are a couple of the keys to successfully accomplishing this goal. An additional key to success is firm management's understanding of the parameters of the legal publishing industry and the tension between providing information at all costs (what the attorneys invariably request) and providing the best information available in light of the budgetary constraints put on the library and information resources department.

3. Strive to provide services to the attorneys and the marketing department that result in additional profits to the firm and then let the attorneys and firm management know that the library was instrumental in providing those services. If library managers and information professionals can accomplish this goal and *communicate* it to firm management, they would be valued more as integral members of the firm's management team and important players in the success of the firm. Information professionals perform these tasks every day—it is getting firm management to recognize their value that needs improvement. Firm management must come to understand that every department, particularly the department that provides its members with timely, accurate, current, and cost-effective information, helps the firm serve its clients and turn a profit. Better communication between library managers and firm management is one of the keys to success in accomplishing this goal.

4. Strive to recover as much as possible for the cost of online research by charging clients back for that research. Recovery of more of the cost of online research will help increase firm profits and will increase the library manager's visibility with firm management. Higher firm profits and greater profits per partner is the name of the law firm game. One of the keys to success in accomplishing this goal is understanding the economics of online services contracts. Both library managers and firm management should strive to do a better job at this. Another key to the successful accomplishment of this goal is a commitment to reduce research charges assigned to the firm when those charges could, in fact, be assigned to a client. Training and education for attorneys and researchers on cost-effective methods of online searching and the importance to the firm to charge back online research will assist library managers in seeing this goal come to

fruition. Finally, buy-in from upper firm management about the importance of the issue and the strategies that need to be developed to be successful in achieving better cost recovery will be a key factor in reaching the goal.

5. Strive to keep current on the latest trends in law librarianship and take steps to implement those trends within your firm. What you don't know can hurt you. Attending professional development conferences helps information professionals keep abreast of the trends in the industry and lets them know what works and what doesn't in other law firms. The key to success for the accomplishment of this goal is firm management's willingness to allow information professionals to attend professional development programs. Firm management must come to recognize the importance of these programs before information professionals can be successful in implementing any of the knowledge they have gained from their attendance at the programs.

Since October 2003, Mariann Sears has been firm-wide library manager for Thompson & Knight LLP, a Dallas-based law firm comprised of more than 400 attorneys with offices in Texas, New York, Mexico, Brazil, England, Algeria, and France. Previously, Ms. Sears was the library supervisor for the Houston office of Thompson & Knight from 1999 to 2003. She began her law library career with the firm of Brown, Parker & Leahy LLP, in September 1997, immediately after graduating summa cum laude with a Master's degree in library and information science from the University of North Texas. She was the sole librarian for Brown, Parker & Leahy, a medium-sized Houston law firm of about seventy-five attorneys, until its merger with Thompson & Knight in 1999. As library manager for Thompson & Knight, Ms. Sears oversees an annual budget of more than $3 million and a staff of six information professionals and two non-professional library clerks. From her office in Houston, she manages the firm's libraries in Dallas, Fort Worth, Austin, San Antonio, Houston, and New York City.

Prior to becoming a law librarian, Ms. Sears practiced law in Houston for about fifteen years, ten of which were spent with Andrews Kurth in its litigation and appellate sections. Before joining Andrews Kurth, she served as a briefing attorney for the 14th Court of Appeals in Houston. The years Ms. Sears spent practicing in the appellate arena, with its focus on legal research and persuasive writing, have been particularly helpful to her in her career as a law librarian and manager.

Ms. Sears is active in both the legal community and the library community. She maintains her Texas State Bar license and is a Fellow of the Texas Bar Foundation and the Houston Bar Foundation. She is a member of the Houston Bar Association's Appellate Practice Section and the Texas State Bar's Litigation and Appellate Sections. She is a member of the board of directors for the Houston Area Law Librarians, where she currently serves as treasurer. Ms. Sears also is a member of the American Association of Law Libraries and the Special Libraries Association—Legal Division. She currently serves as a member of the West Advisory Board and has served as a member of the council for Lexis' TRIPLL (Teaching Research in Private Law Libraries) Conference in 2006. She has published several articles, both as a practicing attorney and as a law librarian.

Convergence: Information, Technology, and Training in Today's Law Firm Library

Amy Easton Bingenheimer

Manager, Knowledge Management

Quarles & Brady LLP

Introduction

Excellent communication skills are a key requirement for today's law firm librarian. He or she must be conversant with information and information management concepts, technology tools and concepts, as well as legal lexicon. One must also have a working knowledge of the different formats of information, and different ways of assessing information. At the same time, the ability to function as a technologist is much more important than it has ever been, because so many of our services are now in digital form and we need to partner with technology staff in order to access those services, place them, and disseminate them in both print and electronic ways.

Key Services of the Law Firm Library

I believe that the acquisition and provision of high-quality, cost-effective resources is the primary mission of the law firm library, along with efficiently and effectively positioning the content that best meets the attorney's legal practice and business needs. That task is becoming more challenging as our attorneys' information needs are growing beyond the reactive practice of law to a proactive legal counselor model, wherein clients demand a lot more information and knowledge expertise from their legal counsel, such as business trends specific to their core company focus, industry forecasts, and more real-time awareness of news and events that might affect the business lines. Clients expect that their attorneys have done this "business due diligence" research prior to even discussing any type of legal service from their attorneys.

Research and training is still a big part of what we do, and positioning attorneys to become sophisticated, independent end users of information and thus navigate the research process as authoritatively as possible. The Internet and Web browser interfaces have made the training aspects of our job a lot easier, and this is beneficial in particular to the legal audience that does not have much time to devote to research training. The ease of Web browser interfaces has also made online research training more complicated, because people often assume that all of the information that they are looking for is online, and that it is all free. Legal information materials, especially secondary source explanatory materials, do not always work that way.

We take a practice group approach to managing our library's collection, and we partner with an individual or a group of individuals identified by the practice group leader who will work with a designated library or knowledge management resource to evaluate new requests for information resources. We are currently implementing a new process to enable us to do a better job of evaluating our holdings from a practice group perspective on a more frequent basis in order to see if our holdings are still in line with the firms' strategic direction, and the practice groups' business plans. This process will be a subjective one and involve collaboration and communication with the firm's practice group administrators and leaders. This evaluation process helps us to meet our library's main goal: we are extremely committed to supporting the practice of law while also using our information resources to enhance the legal services and business relationship between lawyer and client.

Key Challenges of Managing a Law Firm Library

Today's law firm librarian is facing an increased demand for business knowledge; both knowledge of the business of practicing law and the business climates that key firm customers operate in. The law firm library is definitely evolving to encompass more client centric information (vs. legal practice centric information). Evolving your materials to support these two collection development strategies can be challenging, because those client centric resources are outside the standard body of legal materials. We are now often required to stretch ourselves from a collection development standpoint to look at different types of information and try to see their value not necessarily from a legal perspective, but based on how a particular information source will help the attorney to understand what the client wants and expects him to know from a business perspective.

Looking to the future, I believe that it will be increasingly important to be able to provide narrowly targeted information to audiences within a firm practice group. The concept of selective dissemination of information is not new to information professionals, but the turnaround to identify, acquire, and publish these targeted materials is becoming incredibly short from a reactive practice of law standpoint. Along those lines, the ability to research very sophisticated business and financial information in a timely manner is going to become increasingly important, along with the ability to aggregate information for your user community. As librarians we are well versed with the disciple of selecting resources, but the ability to realize ideas such as combining and aggregating resources—i.e., using RSS technology to combine a variety of feeds and then publish them to a specific subset audience of your entire user population via distribution methods including e-mail and intranet pages is both exciting and challenging at the same time. We are currently investigating content management tools available to us so we can better partner with the marketing department to offer solutions of this nature and jointly support the needs that industry practice teams, client service teams and other various business development efforts might require.

An older challenge that is still relevant today is getting the firm's attorneys to devote the necessary time to become efficient and effective researchers. Every librarian wants to see the research process designed and implemented to offer relevant results and be intuitive for their community of users. It is still challenging, even in today's browser age, to achieve that outcome without some commitment to continuous training both by library staff and the users they serve.

It is also challenging, but important, to be able to fully partner with the firm's technology staff so that both groups of information professionals can work effectively together. When things need to be done in a project environment, it is more likely that people can be optimally effective if they are able to work in partnership with an understanding and respect for the differing perspectives that can be brought to the table This perhaps can most frequently occur in projects when both technology and content are important, such as intranets, extranets, and document management systems.

In some respects, a firm size (ours has almost 500 attorneys) may appear to makes meeting these challenges easier because of the theory that larger firms may have more resources at their disposal. However, firm culture is also an important factor to consider. If you have a more individualistic culture, it may mean more customized requests for information and technology solutions versus requests for more homogonous ones. Firm size and culture are important factors to consider in how information and technology solutions are evaluated and addressed.

Benchmarking the Library's Effectiveness

There are several methods that we use to evaluate whether our library's services are effective. We keep a monthly count of our volume of research overall, and we capture our research requests using a technology support application that offers us a workflow process for handling and escalating reference and research requests. This software solution also provides us with a documentation/knowledge base for how those research requests are resolved. Our firm also conducts an annual administrative customer satisfaction survey for all firm administrative departments. This survey is sent out to all the employees in the firm and that allows us to get feedback per location as well as a firm wide basis. This feedback gives us a quality measure as to how satisfied our customers are with the services we have identified and delivered.

I would suggest that the process of evaluating new information and knowledge technologies for the law firm library, or benchmarking new resources to determine whether they are worthwhile, is part art and part science. For example, if the solution is more technically based, we will use a formal project intake process by which we evaluate the cost; investigate if there are similar resources (both commercial and ones we may already own) that should be considered as part of the process; and try to identify what our estimated return on investment would be if the proposed solution were to be implemented. This process is done so that we can demonstrate our due diligence in making a good business decision. If, however, a solution is more information based, we will need to make a more subjective decision, especially if a resource is more specialized within a group. We organize our library and knowledge management teams internally by practice groups, but we also have client service teams or industry areas that operate to support a specific client base. When you get into an area such as one that is a bit more specialized, the decision-making process is not quite as scientific and can become more subjective and involve more human feedback from library/knowledge management staff, technology staff, and a select representative of the lawyers themselves.

Key Skills for the Next Generation of Law Firm Librarians

The ability to understand business and finance concepts is one of the most important skills for the next generation of law firm librarians, especially when you reach a management level. Library science programs do a great job in terms of training students to understand core library concepts (such as reference and research strategies, collection development theories, and cataloging and classification procedures), but library management, especially in a legal environment, has a heavy expense management component in it. Being able to understand accounting balance sheets, justify expenses, and calculate return on investments is very helpful. Being proficient in some of the key business tools such as Microsoft Excel and Microsoft Access can provide you with a mechanism to detailed tracking and reporting specific to library/knowledge management expenses. It also positions you to fully maximize library management systems. Our jobs can be somewhat detail-oriented, especially from the collection management side—and the more you know about the tools available to help you streamline that process, the easier it becomes to provide expense justification. Your finance department will be happy, and you will be happier too, because after an initial configuration of your programs, you will not spend repetitive hours trying to come up with calculations when budgeting time comes around—i.e., how much did this group spend; how much did this resource cost; and how much did that price increase?

I think that it is also helpful to have a very good conceptual and possibly even a technical skill level with respect to Web programming or Web 2.0 skills. With all of the new technologies that seem to be becoming a part of our environment, such as blogs, wikis, RSS feeds, etc., I suggest that librarians will be positioned to do a better job of servicing our end users if we can roll up our sleeves and offer our skills and end user perspectives to collaboration on producing content and interfaces that ideally will exceed our end user's expectations.

Job Titles and Roles within the Law Firm Library

Job titles and roles within a law firm library are always changing; therefore, being flexible and not getting hung up on a label is important. In our organization we have used the title "Information Assistant" to describe our entry clerical level library position—i.e., someone who handles the more clerical aspects of the library (such as mail processing, routing, and invoice processing). Information specialists are degreed librarians who provide reference and research services as well as teaching and training, thereby providing more sophisticated interactions with the library's end users. We also have knowledge management liaisons, who go beyond providing data and information services to work at the knowledge level in terms of trying to understand what a group or individual attorneys need from an internal knowledge perspective. They also work more closely with the technology staff to identify efficient ways to make knowledge services easily accessible and highly relevant.

If a firm chooses to embrace knowledge management, it is important to find a successful staffing model for that service. I think that many departments within law firms may be finding themselves in need of taking a more information-based position to their work. One example of this idea is that within our knowledge management team we have a market research analyst that works closely with our marketing department to support and facilitate the specialized information needs that department has as it relates to business development and customer satisfaction. With a greater emphasis occurring in the area of business intelligence, which can and often does occur within finance departments, business intelligence appears to be more focused on not just publishing data, but rather trying to make that data into meaningful information in a meaningful context. Therefore, they are looking for staff (however, usually not librarians) who are able to help them produce reports that are not just spreadsheets, and which contain benchmarking to put data in context. All in all, being flexible and adaptable to different roles is essential today —and what you do is more important than what you are called.

Training Attorneys: Changes and Challenges

Law firm librarians are doing more training and less research these days; and the research that is being done is at a much higher level. Therefore, it is important to correctly leverage our technologies and position the right tools at the right access points, based on our attorneys' needs. Our goal has always been to create independent end users, and while it is ideally more efficient to position people to do their own research, it is also challenging.

Some of the more sophisticated research tools that are not used by an individual on a regular basis can make it difficult for that person to be cost effective in all cases. Since librarians are doing more training, it is important for us to know a lot more about the coverage and features of the tools we use in order to support users of every ability level.

There is also a much greater emphasis on training attorneys to make them reach a higher level of productivity within a much shorter time frame. That type of training focus is both exciting and challenging. The new generation of attorneys has grown up with video games; they have taken laptops to high school, college, and law school; they are very proficient keyboarders; and some have played around with MySpace and Wikipedia, and some have even done web coding. Therefore, to some degree, they are more sophisticated than other attorneys, but it can be in a less structured way. They understand the technology, but they want to use it their way, and they want to be able to customize it to how they think and how they work. Therefore, our information and knowledge interfaces are more challenging these days, and those that are more successful involve a degree of flexibility whereby the attorney can arrange their views the way they want to see them, as opposed to the way we think they want it. Tools like "My Views" pages on research applications, a "MyYahoo" type approach, and the ability to create "My Site" type views of information and knowledge services are ways to start to address this.

I believe that it helps to be a very good technology generalist in an attorney training role, because the training challenges we face are not necessarily based on generational differences but on technology aptitude. There are some attorneys who are very sophisticated regardless of their age, and other attorneys who are more challenged by today's technologies and struggle to work with it. In a training role, it requires a good sense of judgment and a very open mind to quickly gauge what the attorney's level of proficiency is and what their level of expectations consists of.

Implementing New Technologies and Overcoming Training Challenges

We center the implementation of new library technologies whenever we can on products that can be placed on our intranet, and the steps to implementation ideally include practice group buy-in for both the content and the format. It is always important to ensure that a certain technology meets a need, and not just a want. The worst result of a technology implementation process is to hear the comment, "Oh, that is nice, but it does not work the way I had hoped or expected." We work very hard at identifying value and strive to exceed end user expectations.

It is also important to overcome the hurdle of finding the time involved in training attorneys to handle these new technologies, and it is important to work with your vendors in order to deal with this challenge. If the vendor is reputable and they understand the needs of the group, we can be more successful in partnering with them to create a training program that is successful for our audience. Essentially, the success of any training program comes down to having a strong relationship between the vendor, the Information Specialist, and the audience they serve. In working with vendors, I would appreciate seeing greater customization for my firm, and the ability to have an interface that I have input in, while using their data on the back end in a cost-effective manner.

Top Budget Items for Law Firm Libraries

The top budget items for our law firm include online research services, including premium third-party database services, and electronic/Web-based subscriptions that reside on our Internet. Other major budget items include print subscriptions (mostly of a treatise nature), as well as statutes and court rules. However, we have seen a major shift from print materials to electronic materials in recent years—i.e., online and electronic subscriptions. Electronic materials offer a major advantage from the standpoint of requiring less of the physical space that is usually devoted to library collections. In addition, due to the better quality of electronic products and the higher sophistication of intranets, it just makes sense to center our information delivery in a digital environment.

However, while the dollar amount that you are allocating to your lease for floor space may be less when you focus on digital materials, the increase in your library budget may actually be higher. Digital resources may be more efficient, but they are not necessarily cheaper, and their allocation in the law firm library budget keeps increasing at a healthy pace. Nevertheless, these digital products will continue to play a major role in our budget going forward as we focus on providing very narrow and targeted resources, delivered to a very specific audience in real time. The digital resources of the future will be very niche-type publications that will be very timely and very important—and very expensive.

The best financial management technique, in my opinion, is to negotiate. Having a good relationship with your key vendors helps the process, while realizing that at the end of the day, everyone is in business to make a profit. I always try to negotiate very fairly and honestly by telling my vendors up front that I will pay a fair price for a quality product. The last thing that I want to do is find out that I have overspent on something that is underutilized. It is also important to find vendors who demonstrate a willingness to be flexible. If you find a product that you think will be great and it does not work, you need to be able to go back to the vendor and say, "This is not working in the way I had expected." I need to have the flexibility to change the arrangement, or take a different approach.

Allocation Considerations

At our law firm, library resources are allocated based on two considerations: what the needs of the practice groups are, in terms of providing legal services from an information standpoint, and by keeping a constant eye on appropriateness with respect to format—i.e., digital or print; subscription or free online services—along with finding the right balance of formats.

Essentially, we have taken our firm's practice group structure, and we identify the relevant practice group in each of our cataloging records. That does not mean that one resource has to live within one group, because sometimes the proper allocation process requires multiple entries and sharing of resources across groups. However, we are trying to allocate resources on a practice group-by-practice group basis, rather than on an attorney or geographic basis.

A similar approach is true for the way you can approach library staffing. It is ideal to be able to consider individual skills and experience into making a successful resource match between provision of library and knowledge management services and meeting practice group needs. We try to position human resources along our practice group lines with matching skills, abilities, talents, and interests taken into consideration; indeed, looking for the right fit in terms of temperament and skill sets is directly proportional to success. We strive to have a point of contact from the library/KM team to each practice group. Our challenge is trying to balance the several practice groups assigned to a single library/KM resource so that the partnership can be successful. I generally try to take similarities of work within a practice group and the background and experience of the library/KM staff into consideration when positioning resources, so that you do not have various groups assigned to an individual with needs that are extremely different from one other.

IP Issues

Changing government regulations, particularly with respect to intellectual property (IP) issues, have had a big impact on law firm libraries. Changing regulations, be it copyright, business regulation, or records management/e-discovery, can really drive the acquisition or composition of our collection, especially since the Internet age is upon us.

For example, what users assume and what the publisher provides in a license agreement can be very different; therefore, it is essential to have the necessary skills that will give you the ability to read and understand the licensing contract, and to look for specific language that may be of concern. Areas I have learned to look for are growth provisions and termination clauses. The job of reviewing contract language may not always be reasonable to be done in and of itself by the librarian. In some cases, the firm may have counsel who can assist with the IP evaluation process, because it is becoming increasingly difficult to ensure that your needs as an information consumer are met, while the publisher's needs as an information purveyor are accommodated. Copyright and license termination provisions are two of the most important areas to always be aware of.

Helpful Resources

There is a both a traditional and a non-traditional list of helpful resources for law firm librarians. Certainly, the American Association of Law Libraries has long supported law librarians; and the Special Libraries Association has a legal division that is also very useful.

However, with the new emphasis on integration and technology, organizations such as the International Legal Technology Association are interesting to investigate from a librarian's perspective. More sophisticated knowledge management issues with a heavy technology emphasis are studied by the Montague Institute. There is also a wealth of local organizations at the state level that provide a wonderful opportunity to network and get some key updates within your own geography.

Looking to the Future

As law firms grow bigger and expand to different locations in the years to come, it will be increasingly challenging for law firm librarians to find ways to manage professionals across locations, and to find effective methods of communication based on time zone differences, keeping in mind that different people prefer to receive information in different ways—some people are great with e-mail, and others struggle unless they are in a face-to-face conversation. When operating across different geographies, trying to have a sense for each office's local nuances in order to make communication effective is something to be sensitive to, especially if you do not have a single culture that is extremely pervasive throughout the whole organization. In many cases, more sensitivity is required in order to make certain changes effective.

The need to continue interacting with technology and marketing staff will also increase in the years to come. Everybody has their own idea of the most strategic issue in a law firm—i.e., what drives everything else—and I think that it is important for the library/knowledge management professional to collaborate with both technology and marketing to support the law firm's strategy, and to have a more collaborative seat at the table.

Final Thoughts: Meeting Expectations

Lawyers and legal researchers expect the law firm library to provide what they want—and this can be challenging, because what they need and what they want are two entirely different things. However, a skilled library staff will be able to translate a lawyer's wishes and obtain the results they are looking for quickly, cost effectively, and with a high level of quality. It takes practice and teamwork in order to achieve success when a project looks very imposing, and it often takes a lot of coordination and effort to get the job done, and to make sure that your customers are satisfied.

Therefore, I always advise someone who is developing a library or moving into a management role to be flexible and open to change. You must try to learn something from every opportunity, and you must try to be as forward thinking as you can with respect to learning about new technologies and exploring areas that may appear to be non-traditional, because there is always a benefit you can gain from those types of experiences. Having a limitless mind is the best way to prepare yourself for the challenges of this job, because a law firm environment is a dynamic and reactive environment—and the more experiences you have, the better you will be prepared for it. It will probably take you at least one year before you even have a sense of what this job really entails, and hopefully, you will have good teammates or a mentor who can provide you with a sounding board and coach you as you move through different situations. Patience is also a key quality because a law firm is a unique, challenging, and exciting environment that can both satisfy you and drive you crazy at the same time.

Amy Easton Bingenheimer is currently manager of knowledge management for the law firm of Quarles and Brady LLP. She received her B.A. from Luther College and her M.A. in library and information studies from the University of Wisconsin–Madison. She has worked as a law librarian for the past seventeen years, holding positions as a solo librarian, reference information specialist, manager of information services, and expanding her role in October of 2001 to become one of eight managers in the information and technology department of the law firm of Quarles & Brady LLP. Ms. Bingenheimer has given presentations on using the Internet for legal research for the Milwaukee Bar Association, the State Bar of Wisconsin, and has served as a guest lecturer on digital information and legal research techniques for Marquette University Law School's Advanced Legal Research course. She is an active member of the American Association of Law Libraries and is a past president of the Law Librarian's Association of Wisconsin (2001-2002). Her career areas of focus and interest are in leveraging information services and resources in a digital environment to support the business of practicing law.

Successful Law Library Services: Managing the Balance

Christine M. Stouffer

Director of Library Services

Thompson Hine LLP

Introduction

Imagine a world where the perils of the sea collide with the tax collector; a world where innovative medicines are developed alongside the construction of a world-class baseball park; and where business relationships are forged with participants across the globe. Now imagine a place where you play an indispensable role in helping to affect the way these things happen. Such is the role of the law firm library and its staff. It is an exhilarating ride to be sure, but it is one that requires a precise and artful balancing act. As the manager of a law firm library, staying busy and challenged is just a given fact, but learning how to keep everything afloat is a skill that may need to be acquired. The key services of law firm libraries in the twenty-first century, including collection development, research, and client service, take skill and effort. It is time well spent, however, because the reach of your services extends to the very success of the entire firm.

Law Firm Library: Key Components

Providing a Collection of Relevant Materials

Today's library provides many materials in many formats: electronic, print, video, audio. At its most basic level, the "library," or "information resource center," must provide an appropriate collection of materials. This has evolved over the years and addresses the first part of the library manager's balancing act. Whereas in the past, a solid print collection of jurisdictional cases, statutes, and regulations, along with some legal periodicals, might have been adequate, this no longer will suffice. A major part of a law firm's collection now includes a variety of general and specific electronic subscriptions to a myriad of databases. Fee-based electronic subscriptions may constitute at least half of the collection in a law firm library in terms of content and expenses. Among these are the giants, Lexis, Westlaw, and Dun and Bradstreet (for financial information). However, other smaller, more specialized subscriptions are also becoming increasingly common. Business information resources are springing up every day, undoubtedly responding to the business development and competitive intelligence aspect of law firm research; docket services, M&A resources, private equity databases, financial institutions, people finders, intellectual property databases, have become very necessary tools in the law firm library's arsenal. The selection of appropriate databases will naturally depend upon the nature of the firm's practice. The library manager needs to develop a way to maintain an awareness of the firm's direction in order to astutely anticipate and meet the demands of the firm's library users. This may be accomplished by attending regular practice group meetings, or by asking your direct supervisor to become a conduit for this important information.

Legal periodicals are also an important part of a library's collection. In the past, most libraries subscribed to individual print newsletters and possibly routed it to interested attorneys throughout the firm. Now, firm wide access to electronic versions of these newsletters is more often the norm. In addition to the basic newsletter, these databases often provide value-added "extras" that a library never knew it needed, but soon discovered it cannot function without. I have surveyed lawyers in all of the firms where I have worked and have found that legal and business news is at the top of the list of valuable services received from the library. This is an area which is getting more attention every year, and the one to which the "periodical" industry, mostly electronic, is directing most of its attention and resources. There is little question that now, more than ever, lawyers require this service from the law firm library.

The law library collection still does require some print materials, if only for ease of use, attorney preference, and some client demands. This is most applicable to treatises, loose-leaf services, and statutory and regulatory materials. In some libraries, print case reporters are still available. However, this will probably become more of a rarity in future years. It has become fast and efficient to locate cases online at a nominal cost, so that the era of libraries full of print reporters is doomed to extinction. The amount of real estate (that is, office space) required to house shelves of books is becoming cost prohibitive to most firms. Firm executives find more revenue-producing uses for space formerly occupied by the firm library, including attorney offices or conference rooms. Architects and space planners are well aware of the trend to eliminate print reporters and other books in law firm libraries. As a result, case reporters are usually the first things to be discarded during a law library shrinking exercise. I have worked on several library renovations in recent years, and the common denominator is the increased elimination of print materials. It seems that only the librarians and the actual researchers realize the value of retaining the aforementioned specialized treatises, loose-leaf services, statutes and regulations, among other resources in print format. Managers whose library is undergoing a library renovation or move may need to convince the architects or executive members of the firm of the value of these specialized materials print materials. As such, the library manager should have actual examples of which titles are necessary in print and why. Try to rely on positive statistics or anecdotes. I have learned that actually providing firm management with names of specific lawyers or other library users is a valuable piece of evidence. You may also wish to tie the titles in to a specific type of work, or a very large client whose research depends on maintaining specific titles in print. Whichever way it is done, a positive argument carries more weight than a mere blanket endorsement that libraries have books.

Collection development is something that should take place on a regular basis within the firm. The library manager can use collection development strategies in the following ways:

A. When considering a new title or electronic service, weigh its benefits against what you already own and if the new title is better, consider a swap-out. This will let firm management know that you are managing your costs, and that requests are not mindlessly being ordered and falling into a black hole of expenses within the library. Keep accurate records so that you are ready to show management where you traded titles to save money and keep the collection current.

B. Talk to practice group leaders throughout the year; if possible, every year (or at another convenient interval) conduct a major, structured collection development survey across the firm. Note that this can become a major project which requires much careful planning and execution. You will have to make sure that you have an accurate listing of titles in all your locations. Decide who will be the spokesperson for each practice group. It may well be the practice group leader. If so, set up a convenient time to meet and go through the list. I recommend actually looking at the materials in the library, with list in hand. Sometimes the mere sight of the book (if it is a print resource) evokes strong positive or negative reactions. When considering electronic resources during a major collection review, be honest about the cost of the service and compare it to other existing or less expensive subscriptions. Work with the practice group spokesperson to make sure the best-suited electronic resources are selected. If a practice group leader defers to the lead associates who are conducting most of the research, a word of caution: Make sure that there is no mistaking the practice group leader's intention on who has final say in cancellations or recommendations for purchase. The situation may occur where a title is disposed, only to have a partner or practice group leader forget what happened during the latest collection review process.

C. Look at what you are borrowing from other libraries. If there is a consistent pattern for a specific title or type of practice material, consider adding it to your collection.

D. Study your own library's check-out patterns. If something is rarely used or shelved, or accessed electronically, consider canceling it. There are tools available that will monitor use of your electronic subscriptions, so you can check to see whether an electronic resource can be canceled or downsized in number of users or licenses.

Maintaining a useful, relevant collection in today's dynamic law firm environment can be a bit like trying to aim at a moving target. However, given the budgetary constraints of most law firm libraries and the wide range of materials available, it is a skill and habit which must be cultivated. On the upside, it is clearly a task for which "practice becomes perfect" takes on a very real meaning.

Reference and Research Services

In addition to having a relevant collection of resources, a very important service provided by the law firm library is reference and research. This is a service that is highly valued by the lawyers and other firm constituents. In a law firm, attorneys want answers. They look to the librarians to help find answers to questions that they either cannot find themselves or do not have the time to locate. Armed with answers to their queries, the lawyers then analyze their options and can provide expert advice to their clients. In order to provide valuable research assistance to the attorneys, libraries and librarians must consider a variety of challenging issues:

1. How to make the process of posing a query as easy as possible.
2. How to conduct a proper reference interview so that the librarian is responding to the attorney's query and not going off in the wrong direction.
3. How the librarian can conduct the research in a cost effective fashion.
4. How to update the attorney throughout the research process.
5. How to deliver the information when, where, and how the attorney wants it.

In answering these questions, librarians should consider the following:

Ways for Lawyers to Pose Queries

In some law firm settings, it may be an optimal solution to establish a virtual reference desk with a single e-mail address. This provides the lawyers with a very simple and direct route to the library. The queries may be received by all librarians at all locations, or by specific librarians assigned to shifts covering the virtual desk. You can establish an e-mail or chat repository of questions that are checked at regular intervals by the research librarians. This can work well in larger law firm libraries, but even smaller libraries can establish a reference desk-sharing plan. I have successfully accomplished this at two firms, the first of which was much smaller than the second. In the smaller firm, the concept worked, but the procedures were not as elaborate as in the larger firm. Still, it was the same idea, and it revolutionized the way research had been managed at the firm in the past. I had the benefit of this experience on a smaller scale when I embarked on the idea in the second firm, which was much larger.

It takes a great deal of planning to convert a library from the old way of requesting research services (i.e., lawyers finding a name of a library employee on the staff directory or always calling the same person in the library) to a virtual environment. To begin, try to get political buy-in from your supervisor(s) at the firm. Start with your library committee or a partner with whom you have a good working relationship and who will vouch for your work and ideas. Major considerations include setting the times for the service (i.e., 8 a.m. to 6 p.m.); staffing the desk, perhaps in shifts; establishing a prompt and standard initial method of response; ensuring that all staff members are equally trained, or training some as experts in different types of research; keeping track of all the questions that are received; monitoring the quality and accuracy of the responses. Most importantly, you must make sure that your library customers are comfortable with the idea.

One way to approach this is to take a trial run. Plan your virtual reference service meticulously. When the planning is complete, try it out but still remain safe. How? It can be very instructive to plan a pilot program with a small, select group of lawyers. I found that the focus group we selected for our trial run in the large firm was flattered to be part of this new initiative. The feedback gained through the pilot helped us to gauge the receptiveness of the users. It also glaringly pointed out the weaknesses in our procedures. This tempering process will produce a better final result, and when you finally are ready to roll out your virtual reference environment to the firm, you can say with confidence that it is a tested service.

To those who feel that the face-to-face aspect of reference and research should not be compromised, here are a few suggestions. One way to solve the problem of local librarians unknown in all the firm's locations is to post photos of each librarian on your library's Intranet or home page so that attorneys can link a face to a name. Encourage your librarians to call the customer after receiving the initial e-mail or virtual query so that users know with whom they are dealing throughout the course of handling the question and will feel the comfort of a human voice. If your firm permits it, including all the librarians at all of the firm's locations on a virtual reference desk initiative helps to build teamwork, equalizes the work flow so that questions are not all concentrated, say, in the main office or with one or two librarians, and increases everyone's knowledge. Another bonus is that more librarians are recognized for their work.

Another idea is to establish a single "library help desk" or "research hotline" telephone number. This would be similar to a virtual reference desk, and can be used with a virtual desk. Again, the details of staffing, coverage, etc. are critical to ensure that no calls are inadvertently lost.

Encouraging users to send text messages is another way to incorporate current technology. If you have a library cell phone or other electronic device, make sure that you are checking all of your messages regularly. Mobile and remote-working lawyers will naturally assume that texting a research question to the library will result in a response.

Also, remember that there is no substitute for good, old-fashioned human interaction! If your library still has a physical presence, there are many lawyers and others who may prefer to come around and ask a question in person. You should have a procedure in place for this type of situation. If it is a quick question, undoubtedly the person who receives the question should take the time with the in-person user and answer it. However, if it is a long-range question, you may have a process whereby the person who received the query in person will then transfer it to the virtual desk. However, this should be explained to the person who has come into the library with the query so that there are no misunderstandings.

Finally, don't forget to seek user feedback through an easily found link or form on the firm's intranet or home page. Constant review of the reference and research process is advisable, whether informally by talking to your staff, or conducting regular user surveys. Keep an archive of the kudos that your staff receives, and openly discuss any problems. The lawyers and other library users are clients, too. They are your internal clients, and they deserve the same, high-quality service that your firm's lawyers are delivering to their external clients.

Conducting an Effective Reference Interview

The reference interview is an essential part of reference service everywhere, but in a law firm library, it is critical. The law firm librarian must have a working knowledge of legal issues in order to ask the proper questions of the lawyer posing the query. The following tips can be used to conduct a reference interview:

Get the basics: Where, what, when, where: Try to elicit the jurisdiction (state or federal; trial, appellate, Supreme Court or other) What: Cases, statutes, or articles; civil, criminal, administrative, or other type of matter. When: Try to limit by time; this will narrow the search significantly.

Checklist: Develop a checklist for yourself and your librarians in all office locations. Using a consistent checklist of questions for the reference interview insures standard levels of competency in your responses. Of course there will be nuanced differences in questions and responses—that is what makes for a sophisticated law practice. However, asking basic questions during the initial reference interview creates a good foundation and starting point for research. The checklist can be expanded to serve a variety of law firm constituencies. For example, practice services or business development queries require different prompts than legal research. You can even give a copy of the checklist to the key players in those non-lawyer departments so that they can pose their questions in a more intelligent way. This will help them get the results they want from the library, and serves to ward off potential miscues between the departments, thus engendering a mutually satisfactory research result.

Personal Contact: Even if you have a virtual reference environment where the queries are submitted by e-mail, text, phone message, etc., always establish a personal rapport with your patron. Keep in touch throughout the research to refine your results to their liking. Usually the telephone is the easiest way to insure that personal touch, even when you are using otherwise technological ways of communication throughout the research process. The aforementioned use of librarian photos on the library's Web page can help in this area.

Conducting Cost-Effective Research

This is becoming a burgeoning issue in many law firms as administrators try to keep pace with the increased costs of electronic database subscriptions. Even if your firm does not try to directly recover online research charges, all clients want to believe that the law firm they have hired is using expensive electronic resources in a responsible and cost-effective manner. Here are some ways to make sure your attorneys are managing online research costs, as well as ways for the library to track these costs.

It is a good idea to conduct cost-effective research training for all new, incoming attorneys (lateral hires, summer clerks, new fall associations, etc.). This can be done in-house by your firm librarians. Vendors, such as Lexis and Westlaw, usually will conduct these seminars if you request them.

You can also supplement incoming cost-effective training sessions throughout the year. You can ask your vendors to present these sessions several times throughout the year. Throw in a CLE credit to make this more alluring (make sure that you or your vendors check with your state to verify CLE credit for any training that you offer).

Creating quick handouts for attorneys to keep at their desk can provide them quick reference when they are researching. You can make sticky-note labels that they can affix to their monitor. The rule, though, is to keep it short. Explain the difference between hourly and per-transaction searching on databases, as well as other quick tips on using buffet-style electronic databases with unlimited usage (if you have them).

Using a cost recovery system or other program or software to track usage can show you the effectiveness of the money you are spending. This is the tool that the user first encounters when using firm-supplied legal databases. It should be as customized as you can make it. You can block non-billable numbers across the firm if you wish. Additionally, vendor-supplied tracking services are available to alert you on a daily, weekly, or monthly basis as to the search costs of your firm's users.

Finally, it is important to follow up with users if they are exceeding a cost which your client or firm deems excessive. This can be done via e-mail or a telephone call. If a lawyer or other firm researcher consistently exceeds all reasonable bounds in conducting online research, the responsible library manager or librarian should contact that user and offer more training and search technique. Use tact when talking to the user about how the research is being approached and how queries or searches are worded. Provide tips to the user to bring the cost of research, including the use of transactional versus time-based research methods. Please note that at your earliest opportunity, it is advisable for the library manager to meet with the firm's managing partner or finance department to determine the threshold—that is, dollar amount, of a "reasonable" research session. Make sure that the firm's spokesperson is detailed enough in setting forth this amount as it pertains to a variety of types of research, including billable, non-billable, or specific types of research (i.e., insurance research), or for specific clients that may have caps on the dollar amount of electronic research. You will need this information when you are reviewing and monitoring specific online research costs. Ideally, the supervising or billing attorney will have disseminated this information to the associate or paralegal conducting the research, so that the librarian is not the first person setting the boundaries. If not, again use tact to explain the situation to the associate and encourage follow-up with the supervising or billing attorney.

If your firm actively pursues cost recovery, the law firm library director may become more directly involved in the financial end of cost recovery. The director may need to work with the firm's finance department to set up ways to post costs to the firm's financial system. Always strive to work with finance on this important firm endeavor. The library director will probably need to educate finance in this area, as they usually are not familiar with research methods, hourly and transactional use of databases, and the like.

Updating the Attorney throughout the Research Process

As mentioned earlier, in any kind of library environment, the user wants to know that his or her project is deserving of attention and is being handled properly. It is important for the firm librarians to make sure that the patron is updated throughout the process. Obviously, there are quick questions that do not require as much follow-up. However, if the library receives a query with a long lead time, for instance, a week to several weeks, follow-up is required. Follow-up could include:

- Asking if the user wants to receive the information all at once or as the research goes along. I have found differing preferences, but it seems that most people would like to see the material at a few intervals rather than all at once when the librarian concludes the research.
- Expanding the research: Frequently, throughout the course of research, more questions come up as the librarian works on a project. If this becomes obvious during your research, call the attorney and ask if he or she wants information on, say, the regulations related to a particular statute, or a legislative history which is being mentioned, or a particularly relevant law review article that has come up in a case annotation.
- Offer more information: If an attorney is preparing for trial, you may wish to offer biographical information on the judge(s), or

information on opposing counsel. News items of interest may be worthwhile, perhaps if a statute is pending in the legislature, which might affect your attorney's case, etc.

These little "extras" can really aid the attorney in his/her practice, as well as showing that the library has its finger on the pulse of the firm's business.

Delivery of the Information

There are now so many ways to deliver information to the end user that it is mandatory to inquire how the patron wants to receive the information.

Some examples include:

- *E-mail:* This is now almost standard in many law firms. Be certain that you are in compliance with copyright restrictions, if any, when choosing this method.
- *Creating folders:* If you are delivering a lot of information, it may help to put the information in several, well-labeled folders on your firm's system.
- *Finished package:* If you have the time and staff, some projects can be delivered as a finished product, such as a bound printed report. Executive reports of business information lend themselves particularly well to this method. These items, which are often prepared for firm committees, or business development, usually are tabbed reports containing a table of contents, an executive summary, possibly demographic information, and then tabbed sections with detailed reports (such as news, business, industry, case dockets, geographic, and other statistical information). Note: This requires a lot of post-processing time and effort, so please allow for this if you are asked to produce a report. Another important distinction is gathering and packaging the information versus analyzing it. If your firm library has a business analyst on staff, you may be able to take on the analysis portion. However, if not, I would resist attempts to analyze business information if you are not otherwise qualified to do so. Often, preparing a report as described above will provide sufficient information for your

business development or practice services staff to analyze a business opportunity.

Current Awareness Services

It is incumbent on attorneys to be aware of changes and trends in the law. Administrative departments within a law firm also need to know what is happening in terms of various industries, cities, clients, and the like. The law firm library is perfectly poised to provide this important service to members of the firm. Here are some ways that the library can provide this service:

Meet with your constituencies to determine their needs: Be armed with checklists of questions on what the various groups (attorneys, firm committees, business development, practice services, finance, client teams, etc.) require. Make suggestions when you meet with these groups. For example, business development may not realize that there are free U.S. government Web sites that provide alerts on recalled products or environmental issues.

Set-up alerts: Many fee-based services to which you subscribe offer this service, sometimes free and sometimes at an additional charge. Tailor these alerts to the attorneys/groups that are receiving them.

Use free Web site alerts when possible: Google News alerts are available for those firms who do not wish to spend additional money for fee-based alerts; many organizations and government agencies also provide alerts. There are many sites currently available that provide news alerts, and more promise to become available in the future.

Use an e-mail alert organizing tool: Usually, these are electronic services that must be purchased. However, they can be worth the money considering the enormous amounts of e-mail that everyone receives.

If you still use print publications for alerting, come up with a workable way to accomplish this. It must be timely, practical, and most importantly, copyright compliant. It is very important to stress to the firm at large that the library must adhere to copyright restrictions when using print newsletters. However, you may be able to come up with some useful ways to alert discrete practice groups when a periodical has been received in the library. Perhaps you can create a reserve room or reserve shelf where new items are kept for a week or so, before they go into general circulation or are shelved in their permanent location in the library.

Summary of Key Library Services

These three key services (relevant collection, reference and research services, and current awareness services) are the foundation for a twenty-first century law firm library. There are, of course, many processes and procedures that go into the smooth operation of these basic areas. However, the lawyers will see and value the end result if these basic library and information needs are met. Interestingly, these services have always been the core services of the library. The methods and breadth of resources have changed radically over the past several years, mostly in the areas of format, delivery, and value-added content, but the necessity of these services to the law firm community remains constant.

The Library Team

The basic job titles in a law firm library naturally follow the key services that the library provides. Thus, the major job titles in law firm libraries today include reference or research librarians, technical services librarians and staff, and law library directors.

Reference/Research Librarian

This is a position that fulfills the myriad of reference and research requests in a law firm. These requests range from traditional legal research (that is, locating cases, statutes, regulations, law review and other articles, treatises on specific legal topics, etc.) to business, scientific, medical, and other types of research. The usual minimum qualification for this position is a master's degree in library and/or information science (M.L.S.) degree.

Technical Services Librarian and Staff

The technical services librarian manages the back-end functions within a library. Most notably, those include acquisitions (purchasing, processing, and daily mail check-in) and cataloging. Fiscal operations may also fall into this department or can stand alone. In large libraries, the technical services librarian position would normally require an M.L.S. degree, while staff members normally do not. This is an area that is undergoing almost as rapid a change as the end user reference librarians have experienced. The technical services librarian and staff will find that their positions are adapting to the changing formats of information delivery, which is being handled on the public services side of the library. Whereas a technical services department may have processed a large quantity of paper newsletters in the past, electronic delivery of this product eliminates many of the former tasks associated with it. It is as important for technical services staff members to be flexible and open to change as it has been for the reference and research library staff over the past years. This does not mean that technical services will disappear entirely—in fact, far from it. Technical services will be the backbone of the brave new frontier, as it will be forced to find innovative ways to transform itself to meet the needs of the reference and research librarians, and ultimately, the lawyers and clients.

Law Library Director

In medium to large law firm libraries, there is usually a director of the law library. This person oversees the operation of the two or three major departments listed above. Depending upon the size of the firm and its library, this position can be entirely administrative or can also share in some of the activities noted above. Typically, the director is responsible for human resources issues within the library, including hiring and evaluating employees, and the negotiation and administration of the all purchasing agreements, contracts, licenses, etc., that directly relate to the law firm library. The director is involved in setting forth policy related to the library, recommending improvements in library procedure, strategically planning the year's activity as well as shaping goals several years out. The library director is also responsible for preparing the annual budget and monitoring expenses throughout the year. He or she is the liaison between the library and top administrators within the firm. The requirements for this position include an M.L.S. and (most frequently) a J.D. degree. The law library director must be a visionary seer and pragmatic realist at the same time.

Suggested Staffing Models for Law Firm Libraries

Although the above descries discrete job titles within a law firm library, the variations are great. Often, the variation depends upon the size of the firm as well as its culture and even its geographic locations. Because law firm libraries are much smaller than most public and academic libraries, overlap of duties is often necessary. The nature of the work, as well as budget restraints, mandate a spirit of cooperation among library staff. However, law firm libraries generally fall into the following models.

Solo Librarians

This would be a smaller firm (about fifty attorneys or less) wherein the "library director" acts in all of the roles shown above: He or she manages the firm library on all levels, including purchasing and processing incoming materials, providing research and reference services, training on various online databases, approving invoices, preparing the budget, and everything else in between.

Law Librarian or Head Librarian

This would be applicable to a medium-sized firm (about fifty to 150 attorneys). The head librarian would be responsible for managing all of the tasks above, but would typically have additional help with some of the clerical and other library-related tasks, such as shelving of books, circulation of materials, and fielding ready reference requests. The librarian might have a full-time library assistant and a part-time employee. The library assistant might provide "light" research assistance to attorneys, such as locating a case online or in a book, "pulling" cases to be printed or copied, circulating materials, preparing invoices for payment by verifying receipt of items, checking in daily mail, etc. The head or law librarian would retain responsibility for major tasks such as meeting with vendors, negotiating contracts and agreements, and budget preparation.

Law Library Director with Staff

This model most often applies in the large multi-location firm setting. The law library director's duties more closely resemble the administrative functions described earlier. In addition, when a firm has multiple locations and libraries, the law library director may well have several degreed librarians reporting to him or her. The number of staff members across the firm's librarians can vary from single digits to fifteen, or even more, depending upon the size of the firm and the level of work that the library performs.

The best way to determine the optimal staffing model is to recognize the size of the firm, the culture of the firm, and the role that the library will play. In an "activist" environment, which I recommend, the library is central to the operation and success of the firm. The library is proactive and clearly visible. It does a significant amount of outreach to the attorneys and constituents and even the clients in the form of programs, services, and direct research. It does not wait for people to come to it. In this type of library, depending also upon the size (i.e., number of attorneys), the head or law librarian model or the law library director with staff model would be most appropriate. If a librarian is new to the firm and wants to focus on several outreach initiatives, he or she will have to evaluate what the existing staff can accomplish. If more staffing is needed, the librarian would need to present a plan of initiatives, or a strategic plan, to the administration of the firm. Along with this plan would be an explanation of why additional staffing is required. This process may move slowly, however, so the library director should take this into consideration and not become frustrated if he or she cannot complete every initiative in one year.

If the librarian finds himself or herself in a firm with a very casual approach to research, the solo librarian model is probably the most appropriate. Some types of practice lend themselves to heavier research than others. Boutique firms that handle litigation of a specific type—for instance, a firm that practices medical malpractice almost exclusively—would need fewer materials, and presumably, a smaller library staff. However, a full-service law firm most likely will recognize that it needs a larger research and library staff. This is especially so if the firm has an active client service initiative. More library staff is usually needed to help the firm accomplish its larger goals.

The roles of the law firm library director and staff are ever expanding. The librarian as merely "keeper of the books" is fading, and the expectation that the library and its staff are the "information experts" is rapidly taking its place. Because self-directed Internet research is now so widespread, law firm librarians cannot simply search by taking the first and most obvious step. Lawyers can do a large amount of sophisticated electronic research on their own, including using customized news alerts and other current awareness tools. Thus, successful law firm librarians must always be several steps ahead of the lawyers, able to search resources even the most highly skilled lawyer would never have considered. The law firm librarian is often brought into projects that otherwise were not even considered in the past, or dismissed as beyond the librarian's skills or interest. This includes prospecting, competitive intelligence gathering, and growing the firm's business. Law firm librarians are expected to be on the cutting edge of research and resource-mining in areas way beyond traditional legal research. This even involves direct-to-client contact in some cases. The library staff actually may perform research directly for the clients or populate Extranets and other practice resources that can be accessed directly by external customers. It is truly an invigorating time to be in a law firm library environment, and the future will present unimaginable opportunities to law firm librarians and library managers.

In many firms, the head law librarian or law library director reports to a COO, a managing partner, a Library Committee, all three, or some other combination thereof. If a Library Committee exists, it should be employed to the library manager's advantage. Unlike some other law firm committees, I have found that Library Committee members usually have volunteered for their appointments. Most have a very active interest in libraries and want to be part of this exciting component of the firm. While they may not need to be consulted on day-to-day activities, and probably should not, they should be kept informed of major actions within the library. Try to schedule a Library Committee lunch or breakfast meeting on a quarterly basis. Have an agenda handy, but depending on the participants, you can also keep it loose. Some library committees consist only of the "library partner or attorney" and the librarian. In that case, you might be able to casually stop by the attorney's office on short notice. Other library committees are larger, perhaps up to four or more members. You might be able to handle these meetings at a lunch meeting or some other more formalized way. In either case, you should keep the line of communications open. The Library Committee can be your closest ally and advocate, especially if you are trying to make systemic changes within the library's operations. They are usually on an equal playing field with the other attorneys, and sometimes this means that they are effective surrogates to carry your message.

Skills for Success

Librarians in general must possess certain skills in order to be successful and happy in their profession. Among the most notable are native curiosity about a variety of subjects, logical thinking to create a pathway from query to answer (i.e., liking to solve puzzles), and an interest in working with people. Although sometimes viewed as a negative trait, I honestly believe that librarians also must have a certain sense of boredom with tasks, but with a positive spin. A librarian must be able to easily jump from one topic, one train of thought, one resource, to another. There is a certain skill in being able to successfully change subjects and thought processes with agility. A successful, productive librarian can do these things.

A successful law library manager must possess all of the attributes above, and simply put, be able to manage them all in a flash. If one is a solo librarian, wearing different hats at any given moment of the day, he or she must be able to do everything quickly but thoroughly. If one is fortunate enough to have a staff, the librarian must be able to direct and manage all of these things with the assistance of others.

My first rule in managing a law library is you cannot do everything and you must do everything. Sound paradoxical? I think it is the dilemma of any kind of manager. In a very large law firm library setting, the director must come to grips with his or her own limitations. Do not feel inadequate when you discover that one person simply cannot do everything. However, this is where the art of managing others makes the difference. Of course, you must have talented staff, so make sure that you take the interviewing and hiring aspect of your role seriously. However, once the staff is in place, you must be able to delegate important tasks to your staff members. If you have an organizational chart, you can use that as your game plan. Do not feel bad when you turn over a major project to one of your reference librarians or technical services librarian. Encourage a department head to work within his or her group (which may only be one or two additional staff members) to solve a problem. This accomplishes several things: First, it relieves you of having to micromanage, it sets others up for success, and the firm benefits from the multiplicity of talents that have been brought to bear upon a query, project, or initiative. All of this will serve to increase staff morale and productivity, as well as to enhance the status of the law library within the firm.

In handling the operation of the library the way I have described above, you do not, however, relinquish your responsibility as the director, of managing everything. You must keep on top of all of the projects. Create a working document, electronic tickler system, or some other way to make sure nothing falls through the cracks. Touch base regularly with each professional on your staff to whom you have assigned a project. Keeping staff members accountable also makes you accountable, and you have a supervisor that you must keep informed.

One good way to keep everyone on your staff aware of the current status of policies, procedures, firm initiatives, and library projects is to set aside one day per month for a full-staff meeting which should include all staff members. This can be done as a group conference call. Some tips for a successful strategy are: Keep the same day each month for the call (i.e., the second Wednesday or the like); keep the same time frame (I would suggest at least one hour); have a distinct agenda (the director should make notes throughout the month of items to include as they occur, if necessary); invite staff members to contribute items to the agenda; and always include staff member updates at every session. I have found that this encourages a spirit of cooperation and the recognition that we are all working for the advancement of the firm as a whole. This can help to minimize the department stratification that is inherent in any working environment. Periodically you can invite guest participants from other firm departments. This works well if there is a major cross-divisional initiative in which the library will be participating.

Money Talks

A successful law firm library manager should also be fearless in dealing with vendors and negotiating in the best interests of the firm. This is where the background of business or legal training (i.e., the law degree) becomes very useful (and if you do not already have such a background, learn as much as you can by studying this subject area). The librarian is the gatekeeper of the firm's library-allocated funds and must handle them as if they were his or her own. Do not be too timid to confront or disagree with vendors and work with them to get the best deal. Make creative offers and counteroffers when negotiating agreements, and generally realize that you are in the driver's seat. Law firm libraries are major consumers of information, and the vendors know it. They want your business. Do not be afraid to try a different approach than what the vendor is offering. You may wind up with a deal that will save the firm money, and you will most certainly gain the respect of your boss and your peers.

Getting Along

My mother always told me that you can catch more flies with honey than with vinegar. She was trying to teach me a lesson in how to get along. This is so very true when one is a law firm library manager. In this position, you must deal with all members of the firm: partners, new associates, paralegals, secretaries, general services, mailroom staff, M.B.A.s, medical experts, Ph.D. level researchers, and a host of other professionals. A successful library manager should strive to be attentive to each individual's needs, while being ever mindful of the capabilities (financial and otherwise) of the firm's library. When I became I librarian, I began to loathe the idea of ever telling someone "no" or "we don't have that." Perhaps it came from my own experiences in some libraries of the past where I was given a flat "no" in response to a request. I suggest that a good librarian always provides an alternative source or suggestion if his or her own library does not own a resource or cannot provide a given service. Please do not say, "We can't do that" to your law firm stakeholders. Always try to provide them with something. And it does not pay to sit firmly on a policy when a small exception will make all the difference to the library patron and the firm as a whole.

The Great Communicator

Every manager is called upon to be the spokesperson for his or her area. This is also true for the law firm library manager. Develop a clear, concise speaking style, as well as honing your writing and outlining skills. You will often be called upon to prepare reports for upper management, as well as your own boss. Learn to be brief and to the point. This also applies to presentations at practice group meetings, management retreats, or even your own staff meetings. Less is more. People want to grasp a few "nuggets" from what you have to say, so keep it brief but meaningful. It is also helpful in a law firm library setting to have numbers handy. This applies to many things, from statistics for services rendered by your library, to dollar amounts when discussing acquisitions, to the dates that a project started, was implemented, or was concluded. You never know when you might need those numbers when you happen to find yourself riding up the elevator with one of the firm's partners.

Conclusion

Now back to the intrigue with which this chapter began. Your law firm is most likely engaged in some of the most challenging and exciting work imaginable. From admiralty law to taxation, from product liability to construction law, from private equity to mergers and acquisitions, law firms touch every aspect of human endeavor. I hope you can see that law firm library staff members and managers are critical to the law firm's success.

You can rightly take credit for helping your firm succeed when you manage with intelligence, organization, humor, and heart. Consider the ways that you can establish a viable library center, with a relevant set of resources in a variety of cost-effective formats; develop a receptive way to encourage queries and an effective way to respond to them; provide worthwhile news and alert services to all sectors of your firm; and create a staffing model that elevates every library member to a valuable participant in achieving the firm's mission and goals. This approach has and will stand the test of time, in good and poor economic times. It has been honed from successful law firm librarians who came before. As they have done, we, too, must adapt basic library service principles to the inevitability of change.

Christine M. Stouffer has been the director of the law library at Thompson Hine LLP in Cleveland, Ohio, since 2004. Prior to this, she was the director of library services at Ulmer & Berne LLP and Weston Hurd LLP, both in Cleveland. Ms. Stouffer served two years as president of the Cleveland Heights-University Heights Public Library Board of Trustees (2003 and 2004) and served a seven-year appointment to that board from

1998 to 2004. She has been a featured seminar speaker for several professional organizations, including the Ohio State Bar Association, CAMLS (Cleveland Area Metropolitan Library System), and NOLA (Northeastern Ohio Library Association). She is currently an adjunct faculty member at Cuyahoga Community College in Cleveland, Ohio, where she teaches a variety of types of research, including legal and business research. Additional previous library experience includes the Cleveland-Marshall College of Law Library at Cleveland State University; Baldwin-Wallace College Library; Case Western Reserve University Library, Lakeland Community College Library, and the Shaker Heights Public Library.

Ms. Stouffer received her M.L.S. from Kent State University; her M.Ed. from Cleveland State University; and her J.D. from Cleveland-Marshall College of Law (Cleveland State University).

Dedication: *I would like to dedicate this chapter to my son and daughter, Michael and Christina, who have traveled my life and career journeys with me. I also gratefully acknowledge the dedicated efforts of Ted Huddle and the entire staff of the Thompson Hine LLP Law Library. Without their unflinching support, hard work, total dedication, and insightful thinking on a daily basis, the library's work could not be accomplished. And, finally, to Tom.*

Challenges Faced in the Law Firm Library in the Digital Age

Mary Lynn Wagner

Director of Information Resources

Keating Muething & Klekamp PLL

Introduction

I am currently the director of information resources for the law firm of Keating Muething & Klekamp PLL, located in Cincinnati, Ohio. Our firm currently has 115 attorneys, twenty paralegals, and four librarians on staff. Approximately five years ago, I decided to change the name of the library to the Information Resource Center (IRC). Many people within the firm felt that the term "library" was outdated and that we did so much more than just house books. As a result, I decided to change the library's name to better reflect all of the services actually performed by the library and its staff.

As part of changing our name to the IRC, I also developed new job descriptions and position titles for the librarians on staff. We worked with our marketing department to develop a new logo for the IRC which could be used on all reports and internal communications generated within the firm.

As director, I am responsible for the following:

- Overseeing all research performed within the IRC which would include attorney research as well as the research needs of the business development group, human resources, and recruiting.
  It is a high priority for me to constantly network within the firm and establish that the IRC exists to support the information needs of the firm's attorneys, paralegals, and administrative staff in any way possible.
- Developing and implementing training sessions for the firm's attorneys, paralegals, and staff.
  Over the past year, we have been working with the various department heads to educate our attorneys and market our services by periodically attending departmental meetings for training. We also do quite of bit of educational training during National Library Week.
- Maintaining a balanced budget for all IRC books and services and ensuring complete recovery with regard to Lexis and Westlaw expenses.
  It has always been a high priority for me and for the firm that the IRC budget balances each year. We achieve this by working with department heads to cancel unnecessary publications whenever possible and by providing access to a good

mix of electronic and print resources while being mindful of the expenses involved.

- Maintaining a continuing legal education (CLE) database used for tracking CLE credits to make sure that our attorneys have all the credits they need. In addition, we assist with developing CLE programs for the firm.

   The IRC assists attorneys with locating CLE courses and provides access to a number of online and in-house CLE courses to help the firm save money.

In addition to my duties at the firm, I am periodically an adjunct professor at the Salmon P. Chase College of Law and a member of the Cincinnati Bar Association (CBA). At Chase, I teach legal research to first-year associates. This is always a wonderful experience for me because it allows me to meet the students and talk to them about what challenges they will experience once in the firm. As a member of the Cincinnati Bar, I do a fair amount of speaking and training. I also assist with coordinating and writing the monthly tech tips that are published in the *CBA Report*. The *CBA Report* is read by all attorneys within the Cincinnati legal community. I have been very fortunate to work for a firm that is so supportive of my community activities.

Key Skills and New Challenges for the Law Firm Librarian

Five years ago, managing a law firm library was much simpler. Today, a library manager has many more duties, and they have become more complex. As the firm becomes larger, there are more issues to consider— and you need to possess a myriad of skills in order to be able to address all the issues. I believe that one of the most important skills that today's law firm librarian must posses is a solid understanding of the principles of business. I have always run the library as a business within a business, and in order to do so you need to have an accounting background or at least some familiarity with accounting practices. The ability to negotiate contracts and communicate effectively is particularly useful. A marketing background or a solid interest in that area is also useful. It is important to continually market the library in terms of letting people know what materials are available and what services the library has to offer.

The second most important skill set for a law firm librarian to posses relates to his/her ability to perform research. Effective librarians also need to be able to evaluate and stay up to date on key resources. If someone in the firm asks you to find a certain piece of information, it is important to be able to do the job quickly and cost effectively. Technology has opened up a world of possibilities in this area, but at the same time, it has also created some limitations with respect to challenges in managing data. There are so many resources available today that it can often be difficult to keep up on what's available and what might be the best and most cost-effective resource to use.

There are three main challenges that I face managing the library:

1. *Managing Costs*

The ever-increasing price of information is a major challenge that today's law firm librarian faces. Publishers are constantly issuing price increases and developing new and enhanced services. Each year publishers issue increases which are often not expected by the librarians. Many publishers are now starting to change the way they do business and price their services. For example, with a flat pricing contract, unless you and your firm are willing to accept the associated costs as overhead, it is next to impossible to recover all of the costs. Since my firm likes to have 100 percent recovery on services whenever possible, it often becomes a challenge to provide our attorneys with the best resources in the most cost-effective manner. The result is that digital technology opens up a huge number of possibilities, but these changes also bring challenges from both a monetary and an organizational standpoint.

2. *Managing Electronic Information*

Another challenge when dealing with today's technology is accessing information in an electronic format. We face the challenge of obtaining resources for a reasonable price and trying to position them so that the attorneys know about the resources and can easily find them. For example, we receive several electronic newsletters in an e-mail format. It is important to be able to maintain that data so you can provide back issues upon request. The permanency of electronic data is always an issue for me, whether it is on the Internet or data that we are housing inside the firm. In our firm, we negotiate for free print copies of newsletters in addition to electronic copies so that we have access to the information for as long as possible. When this is not possible, we are at the mercy of the publisher. We typically will have online access but when the subscription is canceled, we no longer have any access to the information. At times, however, this situation is unavoidable. We continually struggle with making the back issues of the newsletters easily accessible to the attorneys. Some resources are currently available through our intranet while others are available through Outlook. Uniform access is the goal, but not always possible.

3. *Marketing the Services of the IRC*

My focus over the past year has been on training in order to raise attorney awareness of the IRC's services. To do this, we try to be as creative as possible. We issue tech tips on our intranet and capitalize on events such as National Library Week. This past year, we used the following theme for National Library Week: The IRC is a "Treasure Trove" of Information. Our focus for the week was on the services and resources provided by the IRC. We used a pirate theme and created seminars for our attorneys, paralegals, and secretaries revolving around the "hidden treasures" available through the firm and on the Internet. We also held a "get to know your librarian" contest and a crossword puzzle contest that focused on the services provided by the IRC. The events of the week generated a number of positive comments from our attorneys and the staff. We were able to see that people really enjoyed themselves and learned a great deal about our services and resources. I also meet periodically with department heads to discuss attending their monthly meetings in order to present on various topics that would be relevant to their practice group. This strategy has been well received and we are in the process of attending more meetings to provide short presentations.

Key Services of the Law Firm Library

Our library provides a number of key services. (See the chart in the appendices for a list of the services provided by the IRC.) This chart is distributed throughout the firm so that attorneys and staff know what services are provided by the IRC. The firm has four librarians on staff and all of the librarians are cross-trained so that each of us can provide the same high-quality level of service that our attorneys have come to rely upon. We all perform in-depth research, interlibrary loan functions, and training on demand. The IRC maintains a catalog that provides access to our collection, as well as access to other local collections. We also assist with locating CLE courses and maintain an intranet page that lists popular resources and monthly research tips.

Our ability to perform research is the most highly regarded service within the firm. The attorneys at KMK greatly value and respect the abilities of our librarians. I have always been incredibly service oriented and maintain the philosophy of continually going the extra mile to provide superior service. The librarians I hire maintain that same attitude. We constantly try to let the attorneys (especially the newer ones) know that they can call on us at any time for research and for training.

It can be quite challenging at times to maintain a high-quality product in terms of our research services. I want our attorneys to know that they will receive the same high-quality service no matter which librarian performs their research. As a result, proper training on using the IRC's resources and locating information is incredibly important. In addition, it is vital to have an open line of communication among all of the librarians on staff. Often, an attorney or paralegal will ask one of us to start work on a project and two weeks later, they might call a different librarian and ask that additional research be performed on the same project. If questions arise, it is helpful to know who worked on the project before you and at times, I will even delegate the project back to the first librarian if the project was complex.

In order to foster good communications, I meet with my librarians once a week to discuss any research projects and other library issues. I also check with my staff on a daily basis to determine what projects they may be working on. This keeps me up to date on what research is being performed and allows me to make sure that no one person is overwhelmed with research projects. This method of communication may be somewhat time consuming, but it helps me manage the department and our research projects much more efficiently.

Another communication challenge in research is obtaining enough information from the attorneys. In some cases, an attorney may not give you enough information at the outset of a project. Later, it turns out that they had more information that would have made it possible to get the project done a lot faster. Therefore, knowing how to ask the right questions is vital. It's also important to know that even if you ask the right questions, you still may not get all of the answers you are looking for! The challenge lies in being able to produce high-quality, effective research with a quick turnaround based on the information with which you are provided.

Perhaps the most difficult service to manage is our CLE program. It involves managing CLE credits for 115 attorneys admitted in Ohio, Kentucky and a host of other states. As a result, there is a great deal of paperwork that requires attention to detail and really good organizational skills. It is important to me and to the firm that we make sure no one falls through the cracks with respect to maintaining his or her license. Ultimately, it is always the attorney's responsibility to keep his or her license up to date, but I also feel that assisting attorneys with CLE questions or problems is an invaluable service. I have had a number of attorneys call me after they left the firm with CLE questions and they often tell me how wonderful it is to have someone available to help them with finding credits and contacting sponsors when they experience problems with their CLE.

In the years to come, I believe that the services provided by the IRC will become even more specialized. We will have to customize our resources and our training specifically to each practice group. It is no longer good enough to do a general seminar on research skills; the seminars will have to focus on the individual needs of each subset of attorneys. For example, we recently presented a seminar on how to research private companies. One of our partners saw the seminar overview and asked if we could present the seminar to his group and if we would be willing to customize the seminar and incorporate some venture capital resources. I believe that the new emphasis on practice areas is a fun challenge rather than a negative challenge. Even though this change will lead to additional work, in some respects, I like the idea that we can customize our services using a practical "what's in it for me" approach. Our litigation and corporate groups are rather large and there are many topics that can be covered to assist them with research. However, smaller groups such as real estate or estate planning can be more difficult to serve because they do very little research. Consequently, we often struggle to demonstrate our value and find ways to help those practice groups. However, when we are able to demonstrate our value and teach the attorneys about specific resources that can be used to help them, it's a great feeling of accomplishment!

Key Challenges of Managing a Law Firm Library

A huge challenge for every law firm library director involves managing personnel. It's important to make sure that the right people are in the right position(s); that they work hard and utilize their time well; and that they have learned to think outside of the box in all aspects of the job. I am a firm believer that good communication and continual training is essential in maintaining happiness and high productivity from your library staff.

The second major challenge is providing enough educational opportunities so that our attorneys are constantly aware of what we can do for them. From a marketing standpoint, it is important to continually demonstrate to the partners and associates the value provided by the IRC. As a result, we conduct training sessions as often as possible, provide research advice, publish monthly tech tips, write tech tips for the *CBA Report*, and issue reminders about the services that can be provided by the IRC.

It is, however, often challenging to market our resources effectively to our attorneys without inundating them. I get excited because there is so much happening in the legal industry and I want them to know it all. Basically, I want our attorneys to know what I know so that they can research more effectively. The statistics clearly show, however, that attorneys are overwhelmed with all of the information resources that are currently available. They will typically spend over eight hours per week looking for information and still not always find what they want. My challenge is to train our attorneys about the best free and fee based resources that will help them quickly perform their research in a cost-effective manner. To help attorneys with their cost-effective research skills, we utilize vendor training when possible mixed with library seminars and tech tips. We advise our attorneys of the costs associated with the various resources and when they should be used through seminars and handouts.

Another challenge that our library faces pertains to the increasing size of our firm. Five years ago, our firm had ninety-four attorneys. We now have 115 attorneys, and it is becoming increasingly difficult to let everyone know what we can do and to personally meet the needs of the attorneys and staff. As the firm has continued to grow, one way that I have addressed this issue is by assigning "library buddies" to each new associate as well as to the summer and fall associates. By doing this, we hope to develop personal relationships with the new attorneys that will allow them to feel more comfortable asking questions and calling the IRC when they need help. This tactic seems to be working, but it also requires presenting training sessions and initiating meaningful contact with these attorneys on a regular basis. Admittedly, this is not always an easy thing to do, especially when trying to balance other projects, trainings, and responsibilities.

Goals and Benchmarks in Library Management

My main goals for the library are as follows:

- Providing solid, dependable leadership for the IRC staff
- Providing high-quality research services to all attorneys and staff
- Continually maintaining a balanced budget each year
- Maintaining a high level of billable hours for the librarians through networking and marketing library resources
- Training the attorneys how to perform research in a cost-effective manner
- Supporting our administrative team, ensuring all of their information needs are met

My goals for the IRC support the overall strategic goals of the firm. I help the firm achieve their goals by maintaining high-quality research services, and by helping to increase revenue through librarian billable hours. The more billable hours the library generates, the more time and money we save the firm because we can do research more cost effectively and faster than the attorneys. In addition, if the library is able to generate revenue through billable hours, we can pay for ourselves. This makes our department less of a drain on the firm and ultimately increases partner revenues. I strive to accomplish these goals through effective leadership and tightly focused management techniques.

My primary benchmark to measure the library's effectiveness involves making sure that we consistently come in under budget and that we meet our billable quota. Those are some of the things for which I am held accountable. I also talk with the attorneys periodically in order to make sure that we are meeting their needs. I always tell my librarians to make sure that they follow up on all projects within a day or two of completion in order to see if there is anything else that the attorney might need in relation to the project. This shows the attorney that we are interested in performing the job properly and provides us with the opportunity to gage their satisfaction. In many cases, if a project was not done correctly, the attorney may not call to let us know that he or she was not happy with the finished product. The follow-up meeting gives the attorney an opportunity to voice any problems and to assign additional work—and this is always welcome!

Law Firm Library Job Titles and Staffing Model

As stated earlier, when I changed the name of the library to the IRC, I also changed the titles of our librarians. If I had it to do over, I would make the titles much shorter, but nevertheless, I wanted them to reflect the actual duties of each person. The titles assigned to our librarians are as follows:

- **Director of Information Resources** – Responsible for the overall administration of the IRC. This includes budgeting, research, CLE, negotiating contracts, etc.

- **Reference & Electronic Resources Professional** – Responsible for reference and cataloging   .
  This librarian handles all of the cataloging, invoices, and routing of materials in addition to some research. She also helps to oversee the IRC Clerk.

- **Reference & Information Services Professional** – Responsible for reference and tracking attorney CLE credits.
  The main responsibility of this librarian is reference and assisting with locating and organizing all CLE courses held within the firm.

- **Reference & Electronic Services Professional** – Responsible for reference and maintaining the intranet site for the IRC.
  This librarian is primarily involved in reference services. She also manages our intranet page and develops our monthly tech tips.

- **Information Resource Center Clerk** – Responsible for updating publications and assisting with routing and cataloging.

  Our information research center clerk does all of the filing, publication check-in, and routing for the IRC. She is also learning to do some very basic cataloging. We have focused on training our clerk to perform repetitive tasks and simple document retrieval so that we have more time to devote to billable hours.

The firm first hired me in 1989 and I was a solo librarian. Over the years, I obtained additional duties and experienced an increase demand in research and a dramatic increase in billable hours. As a result, my solo librarian position has now grown into a five-person library.

The one staffing strategy that I insist upon is that everyone be cross-trained as much as possible. Personally, I can't stand when someone is unable to help me immediately and I am told to wait until another person is in the office. Cross-training results in attorneys being able to call any of us and obtaining an answer right there on the spot. We do provide some specialized services that only one person may handle, but overall we try very hard to minimize the possibility that our attorneys may have to wait for service.

Implementing New Technologies and Resources

Before purchasing new services for the library, we will typically bring a product in for evaluation. If I determine that purchasing the product would benefit a certain practice group, I typically approach the department head(s) to see what they think and then set up a demonstration for the entire practice group. If the attorneys in that practice group like the product, we will decide whether to purchase the product based on the cost and the need it may fill. The main criteria that I use when evaluating a product is the overall cost benefit for the firm and if it will benefit one or more practice groups.

Whenever we begin to implement a new technology or service, I will design a promotion around it. For example, we recently purchased the Lexis product atVantage. We are now promoting the product to all of our attorneys so that they will know about it and understand how to use it. I am combining that promotion with our National Library Week theme: "The

IRC Contains a Treasure Trove of Information." The seminar we rolled out for this new product was entitled "Discover the 'atVantages' in Company Research." I also used National Library Week to promote a number of our other services that are not used as much as I would like them to be, e.g., our Themis library catalog. National Library Week is a great forum for rolling out new products and services while also focusing on some of our older existing services.

In addition to creating a promotion around a new product and holding a seminar, I also plan to station our librarians on various floors for a day or a week so that we can promote our new services and provide people with the opportunity to ask questions. The old adage of "Out of Sight, Out of Mind" plays a big factor here. I have noticed that if you run into attorneys they will invariably give you a project or think of you more often than if they don't see you. I believe that branching out and being available on the various floors a few times a month will promote a heightened awareness of the library and its services. Indeed, one of our biggest struggles is getting attorneys to attend our seminars and promotions. Attendance at seminars is voluntary and the attorneys have to balance training with maintaining their billable hour quota. Being readily available on their floor will, hopefully, capture that teachable moment and provide a good avenue for training.

Depending upon the size of the firm, the law firm library will need a number of different services to adequately serve its patrons. We have subscriptions to a number of general services as well as some practice area specific resources. We have subscriptions to the following general services: Accurint, Autotrack, Openonline, Merlin, Hoovers, atVantage, Lexis, Westlaw, Loislaw, Casemaker, 10K Wizard, and Livedgar. These are general online resources that can be used to serve all members of the firm. Some of these services are available to library staff only, but most of the services are available to the entire firm.

Budgeting in a Law Firm Library

My library budget is broken down according to the firm's practice groups. I break the expenses down further according to electronic resources, newsletters, loose-leafs, treatises, and miscellaneous publications. When the budget process begins, I send each department head a copy of all the publications purchased for their department over the course of the year. I ask that they review the publications and let me know if any of them can be canceled. I also meet with each department head to see if they are aware of any information needs that may occur in the following year. Most of the time we do not have any specific needs so I often have to guess at what might be spent on new resources. As a regular practice throughout the year, I will follow up on renewals and send e-mails to department heads to see if they want to cancel or maintain subscriptions. I also keep track of all cancellations and new purchases for the year so that I can report this to the firm's managing partner and executive director.

Top budget items for our attorneys usually relate to specialized electronic resources. These resources are typically very expensive but they provide information difficult to obtain anywhere else. Over the past few years, my budget has become more detailed and is reviewed several times before being accepted. I carefully itemize the publications we receive, noting how much they cost and what practice group receives the publication. As our firm continues to grow, I believe that more of my budget will be allocated to electronic resources. At the present time, however, I try to offer our attorneys a good mix of print and electronic resources. I purchase electronic when it makes sense and when the cost is not out of line. We encourage our attorneys to use electronic resources when they are more helpful than the print, but I have to admit that some print resources are often more cost effective and easier to use.

As stated earlier, some publishers such as Lexis and Westlaw are increasingly moving to flat pricing agreements. Unless you are willing to allocate the cost to overhead, this type of payment plan makes recovery difficult. If your users are able to take full advantage of the contract, flat pricing contracts can be helpful to the budget and allow you to predict costs much more effectively. However, if you are unable to take full advantage of a contract and you end up losing money, this will ruin your budget. Since I strive to maintain high-quality resources at a low price and keep a balance budget, the flat pricing plan is difficult for me to justify. The risk is often too great that the firm will lose money.

Networking and Professional Organizations

During the course of my nineteen years with KMK there have been several resources that have been extremely helpful to me as a law library manager: The American Association of Law Librarians (AALL) has great resources and excellent seminars; the Special Libraries Association's (SLA) legal division is also very helpful with their seminars and the local chapter networking opportunities. Most recently, my memberships with the Cincinnati Bar Association and the American Legal Administrators Association (ALA) have proved themselves to be incredibly valuable. The CBA allows me to network with attorneys within the community and ALA has allowed me to network with other law firm administrators in the community. As a librarian, you often only see one aspect of the firm; however, when you attend ALA meetings, you can learn about the overall firm management and the issues that other firm administrators deal with on a regular basis. It really serves to broaden your perspective quite a bit.

Local librarian contacts are also important. I am very fortunate that Cincinnati has such a close-knit law librarian community that provides a wonderful support system. I know that I can pick up the phone and call someone for help at any time, including my longtime mentor, Barbara Silbersack. She has been a wonderful mentor to me as well as a great friend and I will never be able to thank her enough for all she has taught me over the years.

Final Thoughts

In order to be successful in a law firm library, I believe you need to be incredibly service oriented, have a head for business, and maintain a great desire to learn and communicate effectively with others. If you don't have all of these skills immediately, they can definitely be developed by attending educational seminars and daily practice. Creativity is another characteristic that will prove itself invaluable as you perform the duties of your position. You need creativity when performing research. I always tell our attorneys and librarians to think outside the box and to work on a project with a great sense of urgency. What I mean by that is if you work on a project as if it were your personal problem (a sense of urgency), you will invariably start to think of alternative ways of doing things and end up finding the information. Research requires that you think about the subject from many different angles and utilize all of your resources whenever possible. This may mean picking up the phone and calling another person to ask for help. Don't count that out! As librarians, we don't have to know it all, we just have to find it!

I have been so fortunate to be part of such a wonderful profession for the past nineteen years. I wouldn't trade any of the experiences that I have had, the relationships developed, and the many things that I have learned over the years. We are in an exciting and rewarding profession and I can only hope for nineteen more great years.

Mary Lynn Wagner serves as the director of information resources at Keating Muething & Klekamp. She is responsible for managing all aspects of the firm's Information Resource Center. In addition, Ms. Wagner is an adjunct legal research professor at the Salmon P. Chase College of Law. She has published numerous articles and frequently lectures on Internet legal research.

Ms. Wagner received her certificate in executive management from the University of Notre Dame, her M.S.L.S. from the University of Kentucky, and her B.S. and B.A. from Xavier University.

Dedication*: I would like to dedicate this chapter to my mother, Marilyn V. Wagner. Without her love, support, and guidance I would never have ended up in such a wonderful profession.*

APPENDICES

Appendix A: Virtual Research Form   **120**

Appendix B: Reference Statistics Form   **121**

Appendix C: Sample Checklist   **125**

Appendix D: Services Chart   **130**

APPENDIX A

VIRTUAL RESEARCH FORM

From:

Date/Time Needed: **Rush**

Client:

Cost: ☐ Free Resources ☐ Call me with Pricing ☐ Be Cost Conscious But Get the Information

Delivery: ☐ Email ☐ InterOffice ☐ Hand Delivery ☐ Phone ☐ Fax

Research Question:

Courtesy of Christine M. Stouffer, Thompson Hine LLP

APPENDIX B

REFERENCE STATISTICS FORM

Open Request List / Search

*Library Staff	Stouffer, Christine M. ▾		
*Requested By	▾	***Requested For** ▾	
*Type of Request - Only Choose One **Popup with definitions**	☐ Administrative Research ☐ Competitive/Market Intelligence ☐ Company Research ☐ Copy Request	☐ Document Retrieval ☐ ILL ☐ General Research ☐ Legal Research	☐ Med/Sci Research ☐ Person Research ☐ Other ☐ Directional
*Date Started	2008-03-04	**Date Closed**	2008-03-04
*ILL Source **ILL Source**	▾	**Date Due**	

Chart	
Climat	_____ Timekeeper Billable _____ Research Billable Lookup
Time Spent (to the closest 15 min. increment)	_____ Hours and/or _____ Minutes
Hashmarks	1 Hashmark = each distinct question asked during interaction with patron; however, consulting multiple sources when answering a question does not qualify as separate hashmarks. If a single interaction contains several distinct questions, each question equals one hashmark. Follow-up questions count as additional hashmarks. (more details)
*Summary	
Full Question	

Answer

Date/Time Detail

Options

- [ ] Add to Knowledge Base for Library Use
- [ ] Create an open copy
- [ ] Continuing Alerts

Resources Used

- [ ] Accurint
- [ ] ALM
- [ ] AtVantage
- [ ] BNA
- [ ] Get/Find & Print
- [ ] Gov't Website
- [ ] Hoovers
- [ ] PACER
- [ ] Phone Call / Email
- [ ] PLI
- [ ] Print

☐ CD-Rom

☐ ChoicePoint (Autotrack)

☐ CHSL (Allen Memorial)

☐ Courtlink

☐ D&B

☐ Horizon

☐ Internet

☐ Lexis

☐ Market Intelligence

☐ Offsite

☐ Other Paid Service

☐ Public/Law Library Online Resource

☐ RIA Checkpoint

☐ Westlaw

Submit

Courtesy of Christine M. Stouffer, Thompson Hine LLP

APPENDIX C

SAMPLE CHECKLIST

CHECKLISTS

I.   **AVAILABLE NEWS**

       A.   MATERIALS FROM THE CLIENT

☐   Press Releases (from company site or other sources)

☐   SEC filings – specify types (Annual Report, 10-K, 10-Q, Proxy Statement, 8-K, Registration Statements, and any other applicable forms)

☐   Transcripts of investor conference calls – conversations with CEO and C-people with forward looking information

       B.   MATERIALS FROM OTHER SOURCES

☐   Articles in key magazines, newspapers, etc. as listed by team leader:

     _____   _____

     _____   _____

     _____   _____

☐   Articles where the company is listed with its peers/competitors (e.g., Fortune 500 and other annual list compilations such as Crain's)

☐   Substantive articles from local, local business, industry specific and legal industry sources such as:

         ☐   Articles about the strategy of the company (M&A, new initiatives, entry or expansion into new geographic markets, new/retired product lines, etc.)

- ☐ Articles about or transcripts of top executives (executive compensation, charity involvement, coming and going, in-depth interviews)

- ☐ Articles about the client's support of nonprofits or other organizations, commitment to diversity, and other public good topics

- ☐ Union news: lay-offs, plant closings, strikes, relocations, openings

- ☐ In-depth article that comes after a brief press release or wire article has already been forwarded

  - ☐ Short announcements or articles that restate press releases

- ☐ Articles that mention company/product as a better alternative

- ☐ Industry focused articles expounding on the needs or liabilities or future of the industry and the company is mentioned even briefly

- ☐ Articles that mention another law firm representing the company

- ☐ Articles about affiliates, subsidiaries (use family tree to list them)

- ☐ Articles about or potentially affecting projects we are working on for the client

- ☐ Articles about the criminal liability of company or top executives

  - ☐ Peripheral articles about crime involving the company (bank robberies, etc.)

- ☐ Articles about deaths of top or former executives or inside counsel

  - ☐ Any death within the company

☐   Articles about small projects local to our firm

         ☐   Articles about any small projects anywhere

☐   Stock and dividend announcements other than press releases

         ☐   Opening stock price; closing stock price

         ☐   Weekly earnings reports

         ☐   Consolidated closings

☐   All Market buy/sell recommendations

         ☐   Only buy/sell recommendations where they explain their reasoning

☐   Press release from another company saying that our client bought/installed/implemented their service unless it is a law firm

         ☐   Only these types of press releases where another law firm says the client bought/installed/implemented their service

☐   Mentions on TV/talk shows (e.g., Jim Cramer's Mad Money)

☐   Contracts awarded or lost

☐   Recalls on products

☐   Agreements – licensing or other types

☐   USPTO materials on patents, trademarks (IP)

         ☐   Applications

         ☐   Granted applications

☐   Client to present at a particular conference

II.   <u>**LEGAL INFORMATION**</u> – (use family tree here)

    A.   **DOCKETS**

        1. COURTLINK ALERTS

        _____   _____

        _____   _____

        _____   _____

        2. WEST DOCKETS

        _____   _____

        _____   _____

        _____   _____

NOTE: Determine whether to track only the main company or subsidiaries as well.

    B.   **REPORTED DECISIONS**

        1. COURTS

☐   Where the company is a party

☐   Only where another law firm is representing the company

☐   Only where specific products/services are mentioned – brand name products (list them)

        2. AGENCIES

☐   Decisions where available

III.   <u>FREQUENCY OF DELIVERY OF ALERTS</u>

☐   Once a day in an aggregated email (indicate time of day) _____

☐   Other (please specify): _____

☐   As soon as received

Courtesy of Christine M. Stouffer, Thompson Hine LLP

APPENDIX D

SERVICES CHART

KMK·INFORMATION RESOURCE CENTER

IRC LOGO

Developed when the library changed its name. We place this on all correspondence and reports. This is a black and white logo, but we also have a color logo which matches the colors of the firm.

IRC Services	Description
Research	The IRC provides research services to all members of the firm. These services include, but are <u>not</u> limited to: • Company & individual investigations • Statutory & legislative research • Public record investigations • Expert witness research • Competitive intelligence • Client development research
CLE	The IRC staff is available to assist attorneys with fulfilling their CLE requirements. We routinely assist with: • Organizing CLE seminars; • Obtaining CLE approval for seminars; • Locating seminars on specific topics; • Answering questions regarding CLE requirements; and

	• Assisting with tracking CLE credits.
Training on Demand	The IRC staff provides individual, group and departmental training on Internet resources and various electronic resources maintained by the firm. Training sessions may be requested at any time.
Current Awareness	The IRC has the ability to search various news databases for tracking clients and topics through Lexis, Westlaw and the Internet at no charge to the firm. Please contact the IRC if you would like additional information.
Document Retrieval & Interlibrary Loan	The IRC has access to a vast number of print and online resources as well as document retrieval services to obtain copies of dockets, pleadings, books, articles, etc. Please contact the IRC if you need assistance obtaining this type of information.
Intranet Page	The IRC maintains an Intranet page containing monthly tech tips, CLE resources and links to the firm's most popular electronic resources To view the IRC's Intranet page, please click **HERE**.
Collection Development	The IRC staff evaluates and orders all print and electronic research resources on a regular basis for the firm. All publications are cataloged for easy access. If you would like to obtain a publication,

	please contact the IRC.
Routing	The IRC routes approximately 200 print and electronic publications monthly. If you would like to see a list of publications available for routing, please contact the IRC.
Catalog (Themis)	The IRC maintains an easy to use catalog (Themis) containing information on all print and a growing number of electronic publications. Themis also provides images to the full text of selected zoning codes, court rules and minute books.

Courtesy of Mary Lynn Wagner, Keating Muething & Klekamp PLL

9010